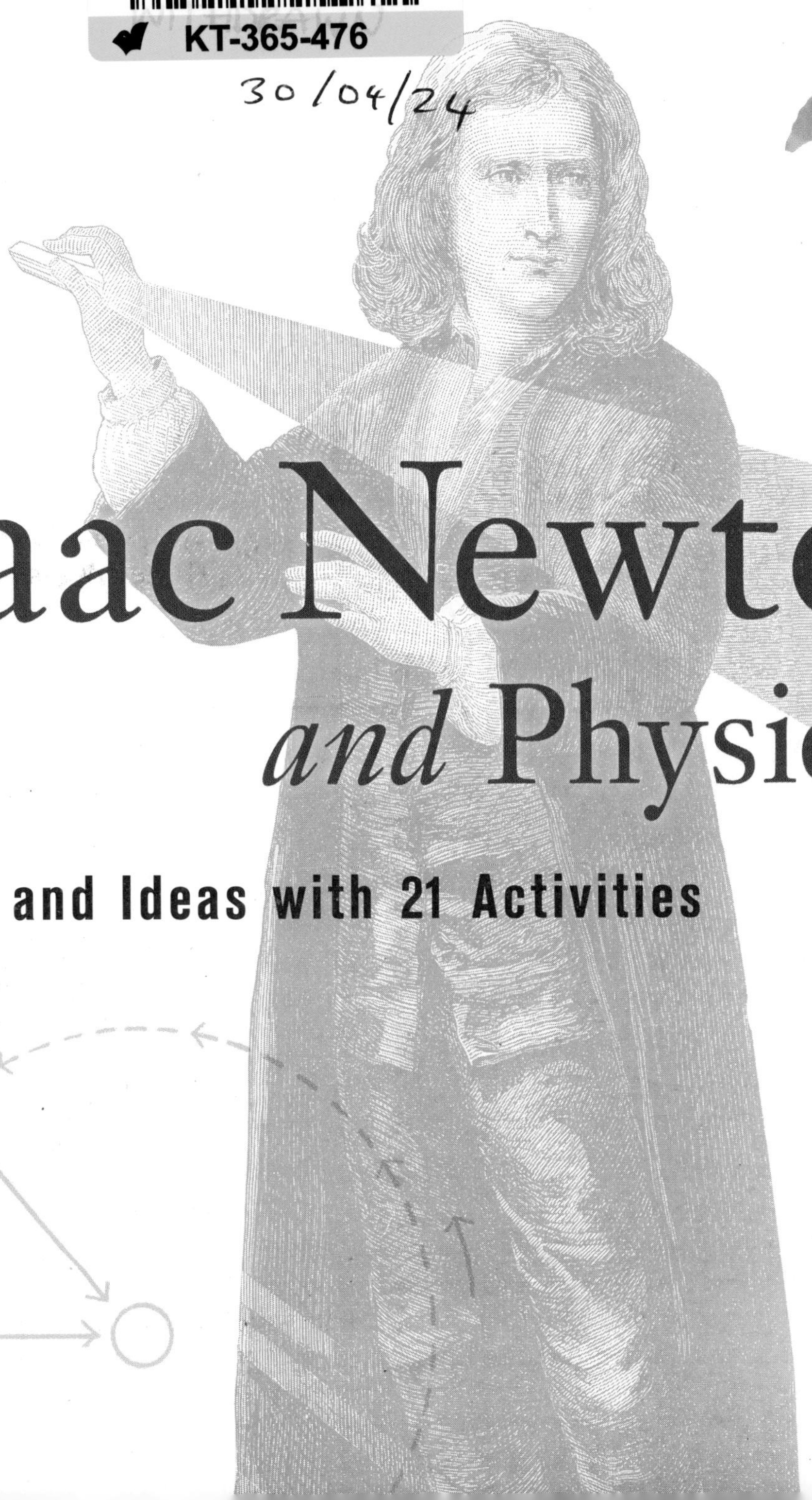

Isaac Newton *and* Physics for Kids

His Life and Ideas with 21 Activities

KERRIE LOGAN HOLLIHAN

CHICAGO REVIEW PRESS

Library of Congress Cataloging-in-Publication Data

Hollihan, Kerrie Logan.

Isaac Newton and physics for kids : his life and ideas with 21 activities / Kerrie Logan Hollihan.—1st ed.

p. cm.

Includes bibliographical references and index.

ISBN 978-1-55652-778-4

1. Newton, Isaac, Sir, 1642-1727—Juvenile literature. 2. Physicists—Great Britain—Biography—Juvenile literature. 3. Physics—Experiments—Juvenile literature. I. Title.

QC16.N7H586 2009

530.092—dc22

2008048635

Cover and interior design: Monica Baziuk

Interior illustrations: Laura D'Argo

Cover images: Isaac Newton: Corbis • apple, prism, Comet Hyakutake, and Newton's cradle: Shutterstock • Tower of London: Library of Congress

Isaac Newton commemorative stamps courtesy of Royal Mail.

First edition

Published by Chicago Review Press, Incorporated

814 North Franklin Street

Chicago, Illinois 60610

ISBN 978-1-55652-778-4

Printed in the United States of America

5 4 3 2 1

To Gloria Lane,

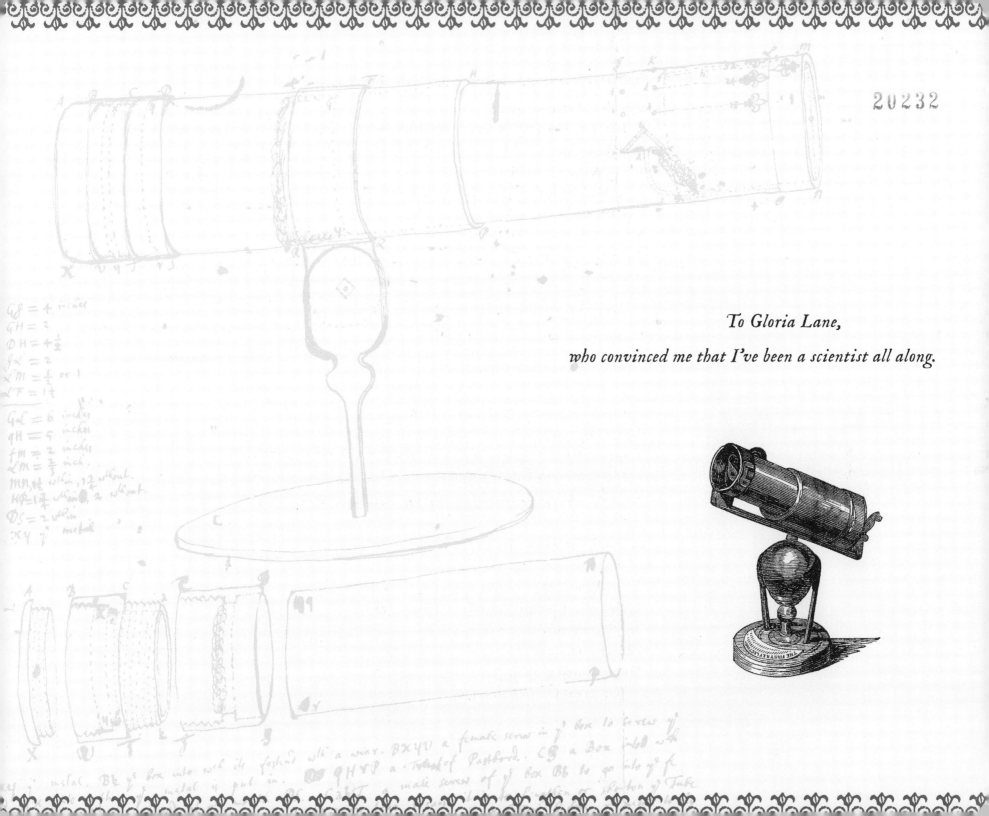

who convinced me that I've been a scientist all along.

CONTENTS

TIME LINE

1642 — Hannah Ayscough marries Isaac Newton, a yeoman farmer who dies six months later

On Christmas Day, Hannah gives birth to a son named Isaac

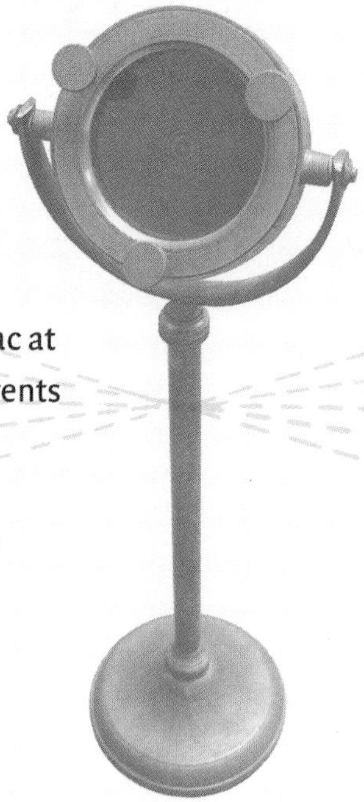

1646 — Hannah Newton marries Rev. Barnabas Smith and leaves Isaac at Woolsthorpe with his grandparents

1655 — Newton starts grammar school in Grantham

1661 — Newton matriculates at Trinity College, Cambridge University

1665 — Newton earns his bachelor's degree but moves home to Woolsthorpe when the plague strikes Cambridge

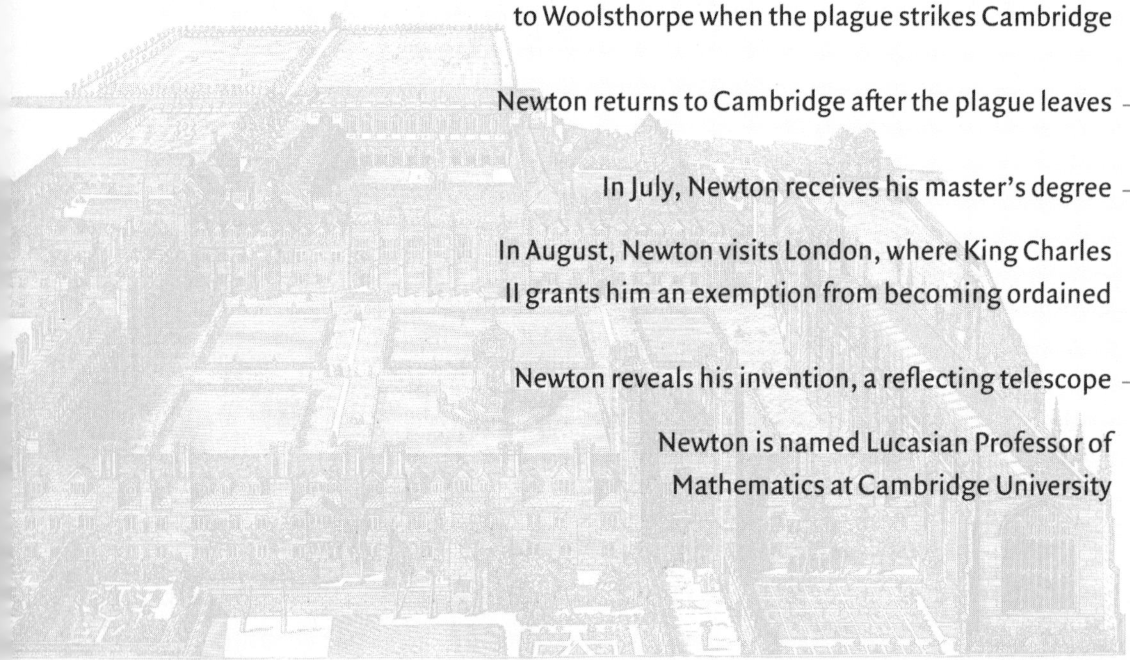

1667 — Newton returns to Cambridge after the plague leaves

1668 — In July, Newton receives his master's degree

In August, Newton visits London, where King Charles II grants him an exemption from becoming ordained

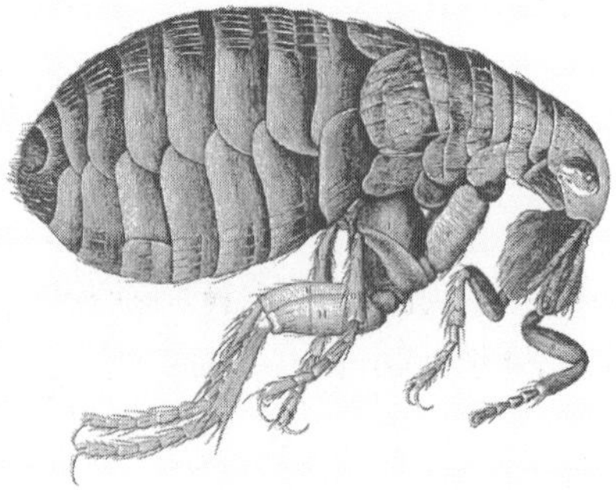

1669 — Newton reveals his invention, a reflecting telescope

Newton is named Lucasian Professor of Mathematics at Cambridge University

1670 — Newton gives the first of his lectures on "opticks"

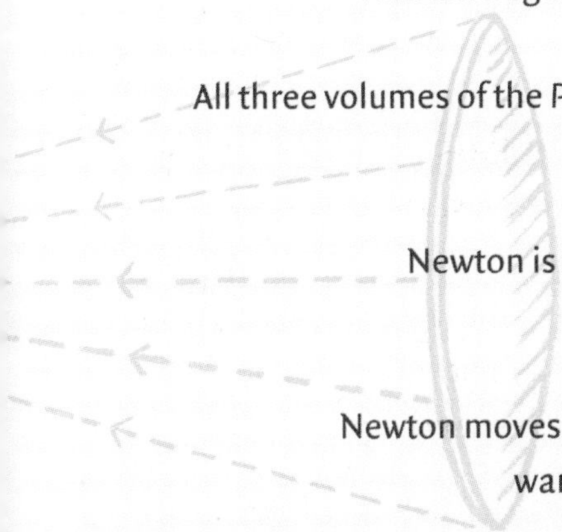

1672 — Newton is elected a Fellow of the Royal Society

Newton publishes "Light & Colors" in the *Philosophical Transactions*

1679 — Hannah Newton dies

1684 — Edmond Halley visits Cambridge to ask Newton for answers to questions about planets' orbits

Newton begins writing the *Principia*

1686 — The *Principia*, Book I, is published by the Royal Society

1687 — All three volumes of the *Principia* are published

1688 — Newton participates in the "Glorious Revolution"

1689 — Newton is elected to Parliament

1693 — In Cambridge, Newton experiences severe depression

1696 — Newton moves to London to become warden of the Royal Mint

1700 — Newton becomes master of the mint

1701 — Newton is again elected to Parliament and leaves Cambridge for good

1703 — Newton is elected president of the Royal Society

1704 — Newton publishes the first edition of *Opticks*

1705 — "Sir Isaac Newton" knighted by Queen Anne

1712 — The Royal Society considers the priority dispute between Newton and Leibniz

1727 — Newton dies and is buried in Westminster Abbey

WORDSWORTH
THE BOY OF WINAND

PREFACE

THE BRILLIANT AND BIZARRE ISAAC NEWTON

ISAAC NEWTON HATED to count sheep: every day, every week, over and over again. In his tiny village of Woolsthorpe, England, in the 1650s, losing your sheep meant losing your way of making a living.

But Isaac didn't care. Raising sheep was boring. He'd rather read one of the books lining the shelves in the house where he lived with his mother and grandparents. He knew he was different. He didn't feel like the other boys who were growing up to become farmers in Woolsthorpe. Isaac Newton saw things in a unique way.

Isaac saw patterns. He saw the rhythm of everyday life, sunrise to sunset, spring to summer to autumn to winter. He saw patterns as the sun, moon, and stars steadily marched overhead. He couldn't touch anything "up there," but still he wondered whether heavenly bodies moved according to the same rules that worked "down here."

Isaac built tiny windmills, water clocks, sundials, and kites, and saw patterns in how wind, water, and the sun made them work. Through his own eyes and the touch of his fingers, the boy sensed that the universe, both Earth and sky, were one and the same. Isaac started to suspect that a universal "something" makes things go.

When Isaac Newton was a boy, people were just starting to give up the idea that the sun, moon, and stars revolved around the earth. At school during the week and in

❖ Isaac Newton's story inspired England's William Wordsworth, whose poem "The Boy of Winander" in turn inspired this dreamlike painting of a boy lost in thought. Library of Congress LC-USZ62-93933

church on Sundays, Isaac might have heard that God had set the earth—and the humans on it—in the middle of the universe. Only a bold few, far away from Woolsthorpe, questioned the core belief that the earth lay in the center of it all.

By the time Isaac started at university, this geocentric (Earth-centered) view of the cosmos had changed. But like every university student, Isaac still studied the classics, especially the ancient Greeks. Greek thinkers rarely questioned geocentrism. Aristotle, foremost of the Greek philosophers, believed that the moon, sun, and stars all journeyed around the earth in their own crystal spheres. Aristotle taught that nothing beyond the sphere of the moon ever changed. What was more, Isaac's professors agreed with Aristotle.

Aristotle didn't think of the universe as a single unit. Instead, he thought that the cosmos was divided in two parts—"up there" and "down here." "Up there," it was perfect. "Down here," things were messy. Never were Earth and the heavens to work as one.

But as Isaac Newton grew to manhood, he dared to question Aristotle's worldview. Newton studied the writings of Greek, Islamic, and medieval thinkers. He pondered the celestial patterns described by Renaissance astronomers, such as Nicolaus Copernicus, Johannes Kepler, and Galileo Galilei. He asked why things like apples always fall *down* when they fall out of trees.

Then Isaac Newton became the first person to pull this thinking into one elegant pattern and make sense of it all.

Isaac Newton was a "natural philosopher"—what we generally call a scientist, or physicist. As Newton studied the system of the world, his physics became the crown jewel of the Scientific Revolution. During this era of change, from about 1500 to 1700, people learned to make observations, do experiments, and develop a formal method to test why things are the way they are.

Isaac Newton detected a set of laws—simple but elegant—that linked "up there" with "down here." Of that discovery was born one of the most influential books of all time, Newton's *Principia Mathematica*, or the *Mathematical Principles of the Natural Philosophy*.

Yes, Isaac Newton was curious—and a curiosity to others. There was a lot to admire about him—and much to despise. Many downright disliked him.

In truth, England's most brilliant natural philosopher was a very odd man. Newton's enormous ability to concentrate kept him working for months with nearly no food and next to no sleep. In a few short years, he made astounding discoveries in physics, astronomy, optics, and mathematics—and never told a soul.

The inner life of Sir Isaac Newton is still puzzling. Only Isaac Newton truly knew what orbited in his own head. Isolated, snobbish, and jealous, Newton could hold a grudge for a lifetime, and he did. Until later in life, he had few friends. At times, he resented his mother, hated his stepfather, and even thought about ways to destroy their house.

With such a bitter attitude, Newton could have failed at everything. Instead, Isaac Newton went further in his thinking than anyone else in his generation. He asked, "How can I explain that the heavens and the earth move according to the same simple plan?"

Isaac Newton asked the big questions. And he found the answers.

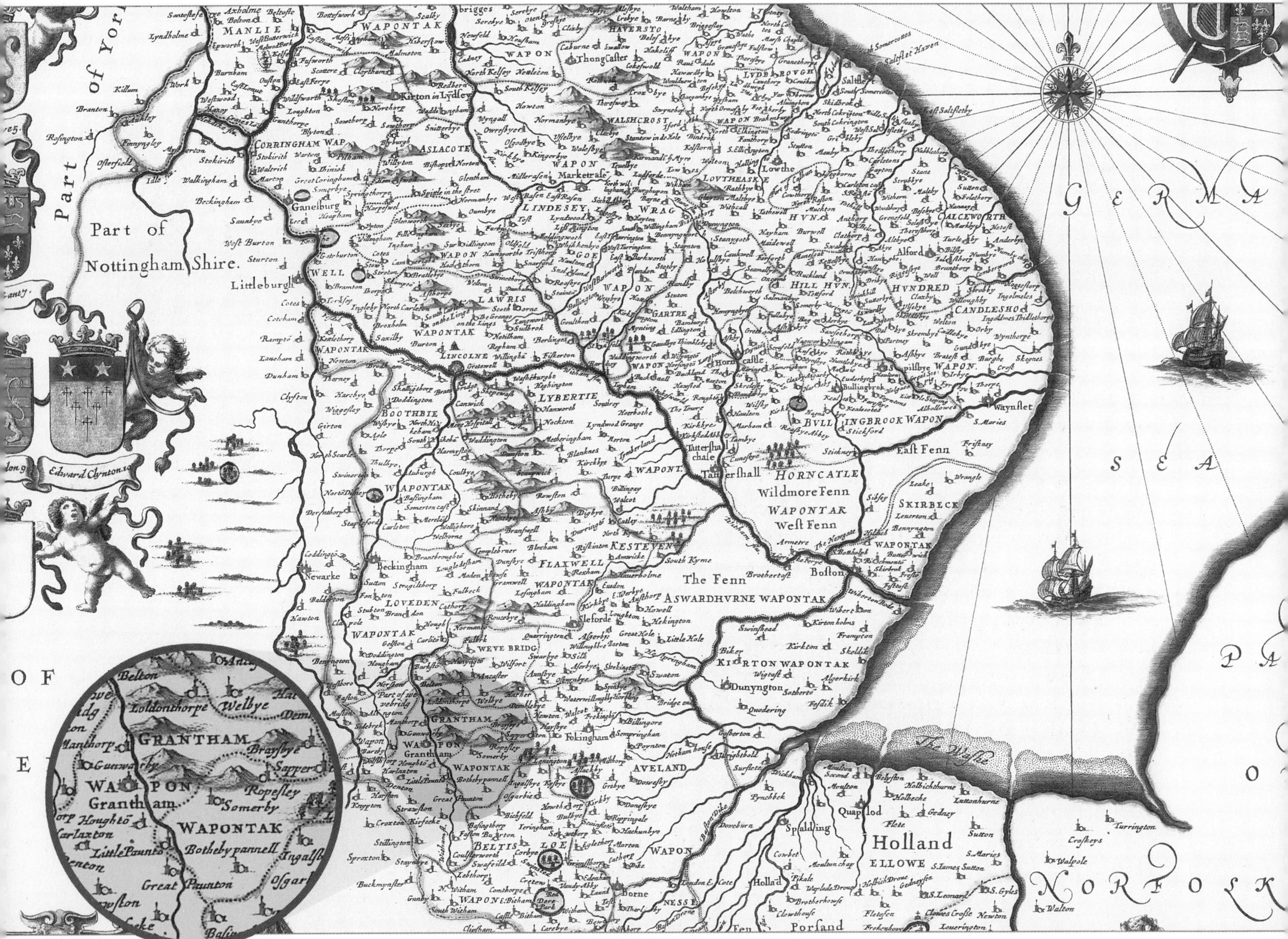
Part of Nottingham Shire
Part of York
G E R M A
S E A
N O R F O L K
P A
O
O F
E
Edward Clynton
Holland
The Fenn
Wildmore Fenn
West Fenn
East Fenn
HORNCATLE
WAPONTAK
ASWARDHVRNE WAPONTAK
KIRTON WAPONTAK
LOVEDEN
FLAXWELL
KESTEVEN
LYBERTIE
LINDESEY
GARTRE
LAWRIS
ASLACOTE
CORRINGHAM WAP
MANLIE
WALSHCROST
LOVTHEASKE
HILL HVN.
HVNDRED
CANDLESHO
CALCEWORTH
SKIRBECK
BVLLINGBROOK WAPON
AVELAND
BELTIS LOE
ELLOWE
GRANTHAM
WAPON
Grantham
Boston
Lincolne
Tattershall
Newarke
Littleburgh
Ganelburg
Waynflet
Spalding
Quaplod
Holbeche
Gedney
Sutton
Porsand
The Washe
Saltfleet Haven

CHAPTER

A BOY LIKE NO OTHER

ON A DARK September day in 1658, 15-year-old Isaac Newton was sitting on his bench in school when the wind began to blow all across England. Within hours, an enormous storm raged throughout the small country. As the boys at Isaac's school would soon learn, another storm, this one a political crisis, was unfolding in London. Oliver Cromwell, England's Lord Protector, was dead. Who would rule England now?

But Isaac Newton wasn't worried about the rain, nor was he thinking about England's troubles. The storm brought something else: a chance for Isaac to perform an experiment. As soon as he could, Isaac dashed outdoors to be with the wind. First, he jumped into it, and then he jumped with it. Against the wind, with the wind, over and over, all the while marking the length of his jumps.

Later, Isaac compared these jumps with others he made in calm weather, so that he could understand more about the wind and its magnificent force. Isaac's experiment showed that the force of the storm enabled him to jump one foot farther than usual. His schoolmates likely doubted Isaac's findings, so he proved it by showing them where he marked and measured his leaps.

Considering Isaac's perilous birth, it was a miracle that he was alive to experiment at all. When he was born at home on Christmas Day in 1642, the midwife who helped his mother surely thought he would die. Baby Isaac was so tiny he could fit into a "quart pot." The household servants who went on an errand after his birth didn't bother to hurry back, because they were sure he would be dead before they returned. All

✤ A 1646 map of Lincolnshire, England. The villages of Woolsthorpe, where Isaac Newton grew up, and Grantham, where he attended school, are in the southwest part of the county. Woolsthorpe was so small it did not appear on the map.

newborns' heads wobble, but this little baby was so weak his caregivers made a special collar to support his head.

After Isaac survived those first critical days of life, his mother took him to the small church in Woolsthorpe, a tiny village, to be baptized. The ceremony, as with every baptism in Woolsthorpe, was recorded on the parish register:

Baptizd Anno Domini 1642
Isaac sonne of Isaac & Hanna Newton
Ian. 1. [Jan. 1]

There was no father watching as Isaac was baptized. His father, also named Isaac, died when his mother was six months pregnant. Isaac's father, according to the tax records of the day, was a yeoman (YOE-man) farmer, a man who owned land and dwelled in a small manor home. Isaac's father used an "X" to sign his name on the tax register because he could not read or write. He also had a bad reputation—a "wild, extravagant, and weak man," one witness said.

This "bad boy" caught the eye of Hannah Ayscough (AZ-kew). In that day, girls rarely received a formal education, but Hannah's family allowed her to learn a bit about reading and writing. Hannah's brother, William Ayscough, probably introduced Hannah to Isaac Newton, and Hannah's parents approved the match. She came to the marriage with her own money, as well. Hannah's parents gave her farmland that produced an income worth 50 English pounds a year—far more than an average household earned in the young couple's day. Why Isaac Newton's father died at the age of 36 remains a mystery.

Isaac's family was not rich by London standards, but the Newtons lived in comfort. Hannah Newton inherited her husband's property as well as everything on it—buildings, barns, sheep, cattle, and tools. Hannah learned how to oversee the farm and the people who worked on it. Hannah had every reason to think that her new baby would grow up to inherit the farm and run it just as his father had.

The name of Isaac's hometown fit exactly how its people made their living there as sheep farmers. Woolsthorpe, in the county of Lincolnshire, sat just a mile from the great road that led from London to the north. Even so, most folks in Isaac's day traveled very little. Many of them passed their whole lives and never ventured farther than a few miles from home.

Baby Isaac lived with Hannah, his grandfather James Ayscough, and his grandmother (whose name is lost) in the manor home in Woolsthorpe. About the time that he turned three and was "breeched"—dressed in boys' clothes instead of the baby dresses that all little children wore—Isaac's life changed. A well-to-do minister named Barnabas Smith, who had a parish in North Witham, a few miles from Woolsthorpe, had lost his wife and was looking for a new one. Hannah Newton's name came to his attention. The widower sent a messenger to see if Hannah would consider marrying him.

People with recently deceased husbands or wives did not remain widowed for long during those times. To the Reverend Smith, Hannah was a good catch; she had land and obviously could bear children. For Hannah, the prospect of marrying a respectable clergyman with a guaranteed income meant that she could leave widowhood, as well as the hard task of running a farm by herself. She agreed to marry Rev. Smith.

But there was a stumbling block. The Reverend Smith did not want anything to do with three-year-old son Isaac. Only Hannah was to move into his home in North Witham. Isaac was to remain at Woolsthorpe to be raised by his grandparents. To Hannah's credit, she made sure that Isaac was financially secure before she left. Under the terms of her marriage contract with Rev. Smith, the minister guaranteed Isaac "a parcel of land"—the same land his mother brought to her first marriage—and the yearly income it produced.

Quite possibly, Isaac felt abandoned and neglected by his mother when she left him at Woolsthorpe. As a young man, Isaac left some evidence of his feelings in a notebook. In it, he recalled that as a little boy, he hoped the Smith house would burn down around the family. Still, Isaac remained devoted to his mother all her days until she died in 1679, even mixing medicine for her when she was ill. But Isaac appeared to have no special affection for the grandparents who brought

❖ Isaac Newton's childhood home in Woolsthorpe, England.

him up. Once he left Woolsthorpe, he never spoke about his grandmother to anyone outside his home.

Hannah came back to Woolsthorpe when Isaac was 10. The Reverend Smith, who was old enough to be Isaac's grandfather, died in 1653, but not before he had fathered three children with Hannah. When she returned to Woolsthorpe, she brought Isaac's three half-siblings with her. Now Isaac had to share his mother's attention with two small children, Benjamin and Mary, as well as baby Hannah.

Like many small boys in the villages around Woolsthorpe, Isaac learned a little bit about reading and writing at village schools. Parents of his schoolmates hoped that their sons could learn enough to be able to read the Bible and grow to manhood in a godly fashion. (Their sisters, if they learned to read at all, learned at home.) In the households of Isaac's fellow schoolboys, there was little else worth reading, if there were any books available.

But there were books to read at Woolsthorpe. When Hannah returned there, she carted along piles of them from her dead husband's library. Isaac must have taken note of the leather-bound volumes that had belonged to his estranged stepfather. In tiny Woolsthorpe, as throughout all of England and Europe in the 1600s, books were rare and precious. One of them, a notebook that the Reverend Smith had used to outline his great thoughts about God, was nearly empty, but its blank pages of heavy paper were far too precious to throw away. Isaac later filled that particular notebook with brilliant ideas.

From the Back to the Front of the Line

When Isaac turned 12, it became time for him to go to a larger, better school. By now, Hannah was a wealthy woman, and it seemed fitting that her son should go to the King's School in Grantham, a larger town six miles from Woolsthorpe. It was too far for Isaac to walk to school, so he lived in Grantham at the home of a Mr. Clark, the town apothecary, who had a shop where he mixed medicines to treat the ill.

Upstairs, Mr. Clark lived with a wife and stepchildren, and Isaac moved in with them. Isaac found himself a friend to Clark's stepdaughter, whose name is lost to history. With Clark's stepsons, Edward and Arthur, things were different. Isaac was smaller than most boys his age, and his odd habits made him the target of their jokes. It was the same at school. Isaac just didn't fit in with the rest of the boys.

Make a Waste Book

ISAAC NEWTON KEPT scores of notebooks throughout his life that spanned his study of all kinds of subjects. From natural philosophy to mathematics, from alchemy to the nature of God, there was barely a subject that he did not touch. One famous notebook was actually a leftover possession of Newton's stepfather, the Reverend Barnabas Smith. Because Newton never lived under Smith's roof, it seems likely that he inherited the nearly empty journal after Smith died. The notebook was valuable—in the 1600s, paper was much too expensive to be thrown out—so young Isaac Newton took it over and used it as his own lab book. He called this particular volume his "Waste Book."

You can make your own Waste Book and use it to record your observations as you do the activities in this book.

YOU'LL NEED

- Pencil
- 2 pieces of heavy paper or lightweight card stock, 8½ × 11 inches
- Pair of scissors
- Ruler
- Paper punch
- 20 pieces of good quality paper, such as resume paper
- 36-inch piece of narrow ribbon or yarn

To make the cover of your Waste Book, use a pencil to draw a light line 1¼ inches from the left edge of both pieces of heavy paper. Using your scissors and the edge of the ruler, "score" the lines. Then fold and unfold each piece of paper along the lines to make a crease. That way, the covers will open neatly.

On the inside of each cover, line up the ruler along the left edge of one cover sheet. Starting at the 1-inch line, mark the positions for 10 holes at the lines for each inch. Take care that they are spaced evenly apart and at the same distance from the edge of the cover sheets. Then punch out the holes.

Hold this cover sheet over the other one and then punch holes along the left edge. To make the inside of your Waste Book, repeat the process with the 20 sheets of paper.

Line up the inside pages with the front and back cover sheets.

To bind your Waste Book, fold the 36-inch piece of narrow ribbon or yarn in half. Place the ribbon or yarn so the folded half lines up with the bottom of the Waste Book. Then take each end of the ribbon or yarn and weave it up through the holes in your Waste Book. You will use a front-to-back motion as you weave.

When you have woven both ends of the ribbon or yarn all the way up to the top, tie them in a secure knot. Then make a bow with the tails.

Decorate your project any way you like . . . and enjoy using it as you work with the rest of the activities in this book!

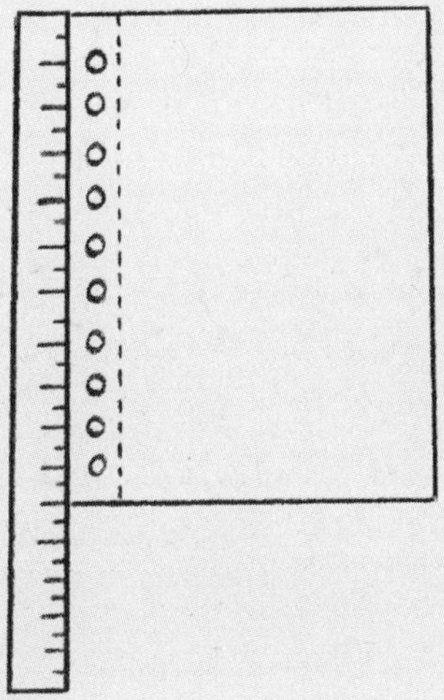

King, War, Execution, Dictator, and King

During Isaac Newton's boyhood, Englishmen fought a bloody civil war. The dispute symbolized the clash between rights of kings and rights of "the people." King Charles I's supporters, the Royalists, backed his government against Parliament, England's legislative body of merchants and farmers.

✤ King Charles I (1600–1649)

There was religious mistrust between both sides, too. Royalists belonged to the Church of England, or the Anglican church. The Puritans in Parliament disliked Anglican bishops because they seemed like Catholics with their "Popish" ways. Puritans wanted to purify the Church of England with plain, Bible-based living.

King Charles made a fatal mistake. In 1629 he dissolved Parliament and ruled England alone for 11 years. The war followed, and in 1648, angry Parliamentary soldiers defeated the Royalist army and imprisoned Charles. They found him guilty of treason; in January 1649, King Charles lost his head outside his palace in London. The dead king's heir, Prince Charles, escaped to France.

Parliament installed a Puritan military hero, Oliver Cromwell, as Lord Protector in 1653. Under Cromwell's rule, life changed. The Puritans closed theaters and banned Christmas merrymaking. The Royalists' fancy clothing gave way to the Puritans' plain attire.

Cromwell allowed Protestant and Jewish groups to worship in England. Roman Catholics, however, were forbidden to practice their religion in public. There was as much mistrust as ever between non-Catholics and Catholics.

✤ Oliver Cromwell (1599–1658)

By the time Cromwell died in 1658, England's people had tired of Puritan rule. Parliament invited Prince Charles home, and in 1660 Charles arrived to the sound of trumpets. King Charles II's reign became known as the "Restoration of the Monarchy."

With King Charles leading as England's "Merry Monarch," Londoners embarked on a 25-year party. Coffeehouses opened, theaters lit up, and women took to the stage. England's authors, poets, and playwrights bloomed. London became a beacon of European culture.

✤ King Charles II (1630–1685)

✤ Pilgrims were separatists from the Church of England who established religious communities in the New World.

Library of Congress LC-H824-T01-P01-057

Isaac spent a great deal of time living in his own head. He enjoyed being by himself, and he spent long hours with no one else around. But he didn't waste time. Isaac liked to use his hands and was a gifted artist. Mr. Clark did not mind that Isaac decorated the walls of his room on the house's top floor with fanciful drawings of beasts and people like King Charles I, the most famous man in England, and Isaac's schoolmaster, Mr. Henry Stokes.

Isaac also liked to make complex models of mechanical objects like clocks and watermills. He planned and built a clock operated by water power that hung in the Clark's home. In Mr. Clark's shop on the ground floor of his house, Isaac watched how the apothecary combined chemicals to create new substances.

When the town of Grantham erected its first windmill, Isaac built a small replica of it. Isaac hitched up a mouse to the contraption, named it "The Miller," and watched it make the mill wheel turn. Not only did Isaac build little models, he made his own tiny tools to aid him in his handiwork. He liked Clark's stepdaughter and her friends and "would frequently make little tables, cupboards & other utensils for her & her playfellows, to set their babys & trinkets on," as one storyteller recalled. The girls must have thought Isaac a very talented boy when he built a four-wheeled cart he could sit in and crank to make it move.

Despite his cleverness at making things, Isaac appeared to have few gifts for schoolwork. At school in Grantham, boys were

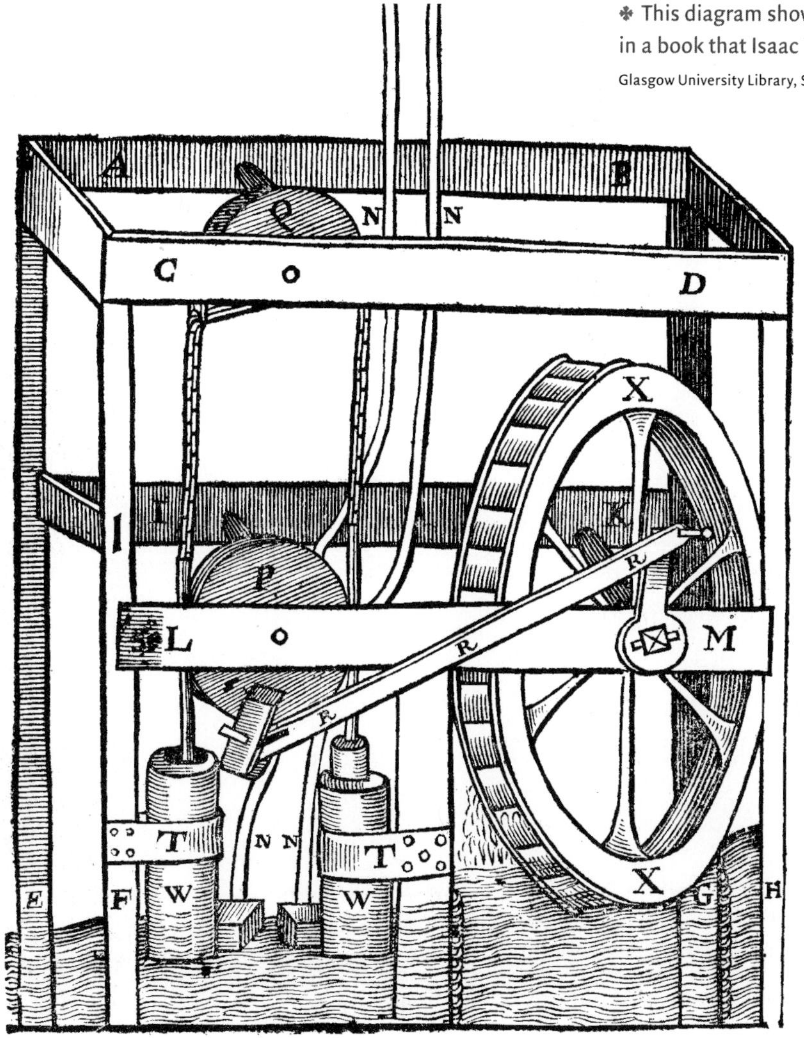

✤ This diagram shows a watermill as it appeared in a book that Isaac Newton might have read.
Glasgow University Library, Special Collections Dept.

Build a Waterwheel

AS A LITTLE boy, Isaac Newton watched how mills used water power from streams and rivers to grind grain into flour. Then he made small models of them to see for himself how they worked.

Just like Isaac, you can build your own model of a waterwheel and test it to see how much it can lift. (Unlike Isaac, you won't need to catch a mouse in the process!)

Adult supervision required

YOU'LL NEED

- Plastic cup
- Marker
- Ruler
- Scissors
- Duct tape
- Sturdy plastic straw
- Empty spool of thread
- 2-liter plastic soda bottle
- Heavy thread or dental floss
- Paper clip or a small alligator clip
- Washers, or weights with holes in them

To build your waterwheel, start by making six blades for the wheel. From the plastic cup, cut out six rectangles. Each rectangle should measure 2½ inches long by 1¼ inches wide. Use the marker to make cutting lines.

Cut 12 pieces of duct tape, each ½ inch wide by 2½ inches long. Tape the long edge of each plastic blade to the spool. Space the blades an equal distance apart, and set each one at the same angle. Be sure that they all curve in the same direction.

Insert the straw through the spool and use duct tape to secure it at both ends of the spool.

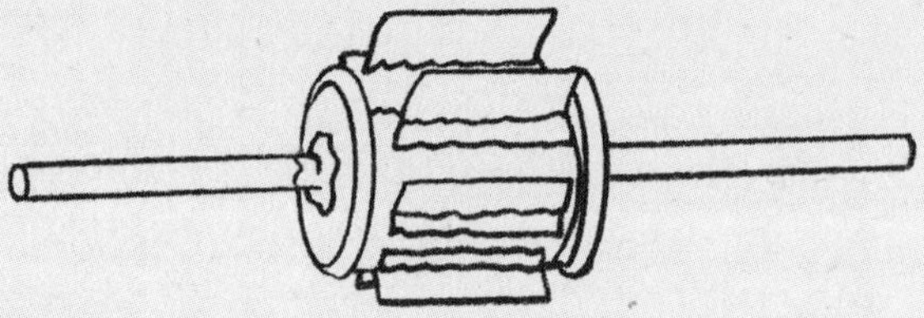

You will need an adult to help you with this step. Plastic bottles are tougher to cut than you may think! Cut the top off the empty 2-liter soda bottle to make a tall cylinder. Cut a small triangular notch on one side of the cylinder and one the same size exactly across from it. Then punch several drain holes around the bottle about one inch from the bottom.

Place the axles of your waterwheel into the notches on the tall cylinder. On one end of the straw, make two 1–2-inch cuts opposite each other.

Cut a piece of heavy thread or dental floss about 15 inches long. Use a thin strip of duct tape. Pull one end through the cut ends of the long straw and use a thin strip of duct tape to secure it. Attach the other end to the paper clip, and hang a washer or weight from the clip.

Place your waterwheel in the sink so that the weight hangs loose. Now, trickle enough water to get your wheel going. Does the waterwheel lift the washer? How much water power do you need? Will your waterwheel lift two or three washers?

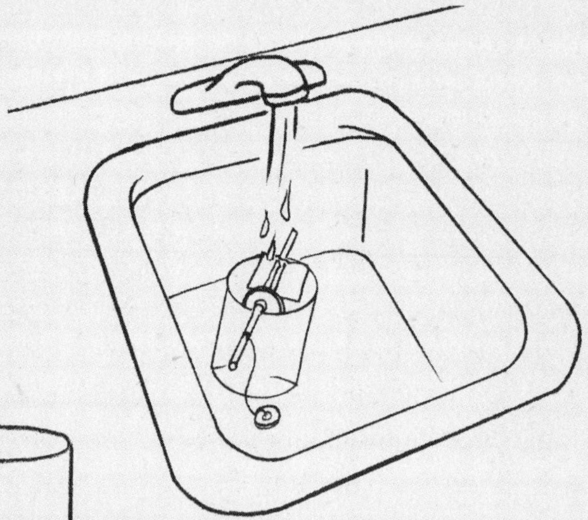

ranked by their grades. Isaac stood near the end of the line. Things changed, however, after a student ahead of him gave Isaac a strong kick in the stomach that sent him reeling. Isaac took his revenge, launching a pattern that he followed for the rest of his life. Isaac called out his attacker in the schoolyard, beat him up, and threw the other boy into the wall of a church. Isaac Newton never allowed anyone to take him for a fool.

Then Isaac got even with the rest of the boys in another way. He took a serious look at his schoolwork and decided that his place should be at the head of line. To become "head boy" at King's School would be sweet revenge, and Isaac won the coveted spot. Now he wanted to learn everything he could. He mastered Latin, the language that well-educated people both wrote and spoke all across Europe. He studied Greek so that he could know more about the works of scholars like Socrates, Plato, and Aristotle.

Isaac also learned basic arithmetic and possibly a bit of multiplication and division. Algebra and geometry weren't part of the curriculum at the King's School. Mathematics wasn't considered an important subject when Isaac went there, and only tradesmen like carpenters and shipbuilders studied geometry. However, once Henry Stokes, the schoolmaster, saw Isaac's gifts, he very well might have tutored Isaac in all the math he knew.

Isaac also learned "shortwriting," a type of shorthand writing similar to today's text messages. During a time when students used quill pens and dipped them into ink—often with messy results—shortwriting proved useful in writing letters and taking down

✤ An illustration from *The Illustrated London News*, October 2, 1858, depicts "the inauguration of the statue of Sir Isaac Newton at Grantham."

MAKE YOUR OWN INK, AND WRITE WITH IT

ISAAC NEWTON'S RECIPE for ink called for ingredients provided by Mother Nature—galls, gum arabic, beer or ale, and "copperas":

> To make excellent Ink.
>
> ½lb of Galls cut in pieces or grosly beaten, ¼lb of Gumm Arabick cut or broken. Put 'em into a Quart of strong beer or Ale. Let 'em stand a month stopt up, stirring them now & then. At the. end of the moneth put in 1 or 1½ of copperas (Too much copperas makes the ink apt to turn yellow.) Stir it & use it. Stop it up for some time with a paper prickt full of holes & let it stand in the sunn. When you take out ink put in so much strong beer & it will endure many years. Water makes it apt to mold. Wine does not. The air also if it stand open inclines it to mold.
> With this Ink new made I wrote this.

"Galls" are oak galls, parasitic lumps that grow on oak trees and are filled with tannin, an acid that's found in wine and tea. "Gumm Arabick" (gum arabic) is a type of thickener taken from the gum of the acacia tree. "Copperas" is a compound of iron and sulfur. You probably don't have oak galls and gum arabic at home, but you can make your own ink and use it to practice writing just like girls and boys did in Newton's day.

Adult supervision required

YOU'LL NEED

- 12 walnuts
- Cutting board
- Saucepan
- Strainer
- Shallow container with a lid
- ¼ teaspoon vinegar
- Pen with an old-fashioned tip (calligraphy materials can be found in art stores)
- Scrap writing paper
- Waste Book (see page 5)
- Old sock
- Hammer
- Water

1. Crack open the walnuts and remove the nutmeats. (You can eat these or use them in another recipe.)

2. Put the walnut shells in the toe of the old sock.

3. Smash the walnuts against the cutting board by hammering the sock.

4. Place the walnut shells in the saucepan and barely cover them with water.

5. Heat the water until it simmers by bubbling just around the edge of the pan. Simmer for 30 minutes.

6. Turn off the heat and let the walnut shells steep in the liquid overnight.

7. Pour the liquid through the strainer into the container.

8. Add the vinegar.

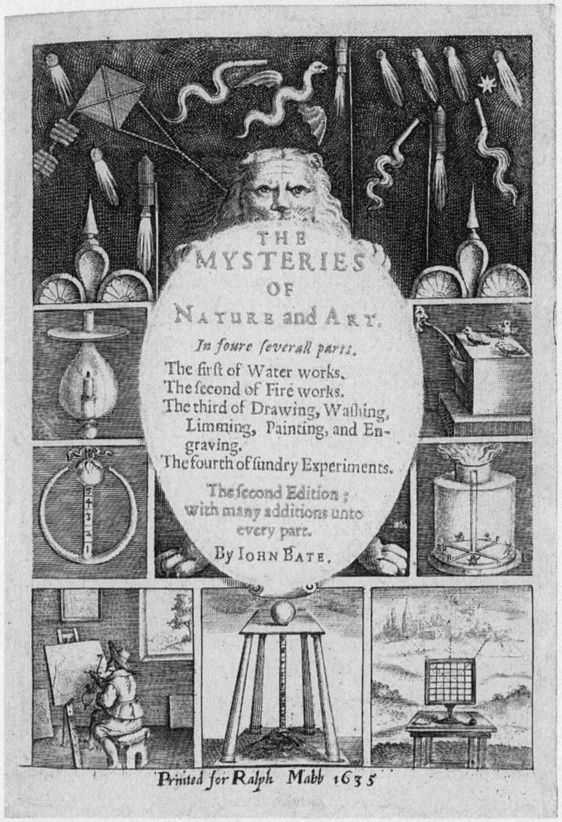

Isaac Newton had access to a copy of *The Mysteries of Nature and Art* from which he learned how to make ink.
Glasgow University Library, Special Collections Dept.

You are now ready to write with your ink. Dip your pen carefully into the ink and practice writing on some scrap paper. This isn't as easy as it sounds. After some practice, you'll be ready to write a few sentences in your Waste Book.

BEWARE: This ink will stain your fingers and clothes. Be careful when you use it!

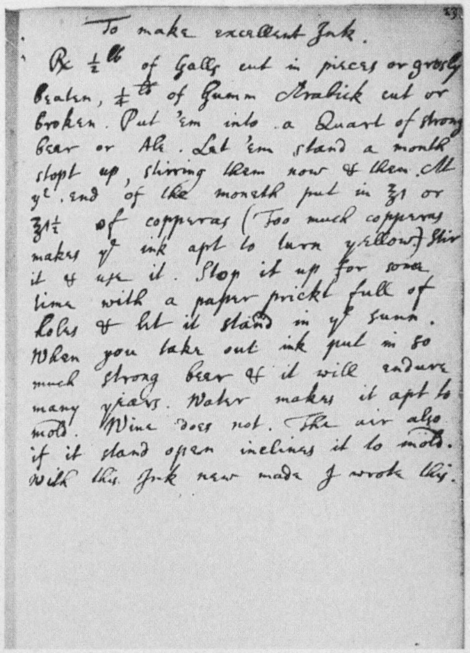
To make excellent Ink.
Rx ½lb of Galls cut in pieces or grossly beaten, ½lb of Gumm Arabick cut or broken. Put 'em into a Quart of strong Beer or Ale. Let 'em stand a month stopt up, stirring them now & then. At ye end of the month put in ℥1 or ℥1½ of copperas (Too much copperas makes ye ink apt to turn yellow) Stir it & use it. Stop it up for some time with a paper prickt full of holes & let it stand in ye Sunn. When you take out ink put in so much strong beer & it will endure many years. Water makes it apt to mold. Wine does not. The air also if it stand open inclines it to mold. With this Ink new made I wrote this.

✤ Isaac tries out his new ink in this notebook entry, "To Make Excellent Ink."

The Chymistry of Isaac Newton, Indiana University

notes from books. The English that Isaac and his schoolfellows wrote also looked and sounded different than today's English. He used terms like "ye" for "the," "yt" for "that," "wch" for "which," and "yn" for "than."

Isaac spelled words differently as well. In one of his notebooks, a heading read:

Of ye Sunn Starrs & Plannets & Comets.

In that notebook, he wrote a recipe for making gold-colored ink:

How to write a gold colour.
Take a new laid egg, make a hole at one end & let out the substance then take the yolk without the white, & four times soe much quicksilver [mercury] *in quantitie as of the former grind them well together & put them into the shell stop the hole thereof with chalk & the white of an egg then lay it under a hen that sitt with 6 more for the space of 3 wekes* [weeks], *then break it up & write with it.*

Isaac went to school in a town where many people couldn't read at all. Most of his fellow citizens in England lived simple lives and did not ask many questions about the world around them. Most did not have clocks to mark the passing of each day, so they used the sun's position in the sky to get a rough idea of the time. Some households had hourglasses filled with sand that supplied a means of measuring time. If there was an emergency, someone had to ring the bells in the church tower to alert everyone in the area.

By the time Isaac was born, educated people had accepted the idea that the world was round, but some refused to believe that the earth orbited the sun. People lived close to the rhythms of the earth. Why would their eyes lie to them? They could see for themselves that the sun rose in the east, tracked across the sky, and set in the west.

Still, some ideas were beginning to change. A few people looked at the world with a fresh view. Isaac Newton was one of them. He started to experiment with things that interested him, to observe and measure them. For instance, Isaac watched as sunshine poured against a wall of his house and saw how the light shifted from day to day and week to week. He marked the stream of light with pegs in the wall, adjusting them as the days grew longer in the spring and shorter in the fall. Over time, Isaac created a fairly accurate sundial, and passersby could tell the time by "Isaac's dyal."

Isaac's neighbors were superstitious. If twin calves were born on a farm, it was a sign of God's anger. If a black cat crossed their paths, certainly it was time to say a prayer for good fortune. If a comet appeared in the night sky, surely bad luck would follow. England's history had "proved" this in 1066, when a comet appeared. Shortly thereafter, Harold, King of the Anglo-Saxons in England, was slaughtered during the Battle of Hastings. Harold's enemy William the Conqueror, along with William's fellow Normans from France, overran the country and changed England forever.

Sometimes Isaac used this kind of knowledge to make mischief. At least once, he managed to frighten a good number of people when he built some kites, tied candlelit lanterns to their tails, and flew them at night. Many of the townsfolk thought they were seeing comets and feared the worst.

ISAAC NEWTON

"Homes of Famous Men"
WOOLSTHORPE MANOR, NEAR GRANTHAM, THE BIRTHPLACE OF SIR ISAAC NEWTON
Driven from Cambridge by the plague in 1665, it was while sitting alone in this garden that the idea of universal gravitation occurred to the young Isaac Newton—the result, it is said, of seeing an apple fall to the ground. Later in life he elaborated this discovery into his famous Law.
Portrait by courtesy of The National Portrait Gallery.
Ty.phoo Series of 25
No. 15

✤ Just like baseball cards and other kinds of sports and game items, cards featuring Isaac Newton were popular with collectors early in the 1900s. The cigarette card (LEFT) shows young Isaac building a model windmill. The tea card (BELOW) shows Newton as an older man, as well as his Woolsthorpe home.

A Farming Failure

In the late 1650s, when Isaac was in his mid-teens, his mother called him home from Grantham. Hannah thought that Isaac had learned quite enough at the King's School and was ready to manage her land. There were sheep and cattle to raise, hay to rake, buildings and fences to mend, and servants to manage. All of this was a big responsibility, and Hannah Newton firmly believed that it was time for Isaac to take on his duties as a future landowner.

It didn't take long for the servants to see that Isaac Newton was no sheep farmer. He sat under hedges and read books when he should have been looking after his animals. When he and a servant went to market in Grantham, Isaac spent the day with his

❖ The Bayeux Tapestry shows the comet that predicted bad luck for King Harold of the Anglo-Saxons. A group of women, possibly nuns, put every stitch in by hand on long linen cloths. The story of William the Conqueror's invasion unfolds along the tapestry scene by scene.

A King and His College

Newton joined Trinity College in June 1661 when he signed the *matricula*, a student roster. Trinity owed its fortune to its founder, the notorious King Henry VIII.

Henry VIII, best known today because he had six wives, grew up as a Roman Catholic and pledged his loyalty to the Church's leader, the Pope. However, in 1531, he broke with the Catholic Church when the Pope would not grant him a divorce. Henry wanted a son, and his first wife, Catherine of Aragon, provided him with a daughter.

Henry needed to divorce Catherine in order to marry Anne Boleyn, who had caught his eye at the Royal Court. The Pope said no. Divorce went against Church law, even if it was the King who wanted one. So Henry established his own Church of England. He named himself its "supreme head" and granted himself the divorce. Then he married Anne, who gave him a daughter as well.

In search of wealth to run England, Henry destroyed Catholic churches and monasteries and took their riches for the Crown. Then his attention turned to wealthy universities like Cambridge and Oxford. Stories circulated in Cambridge that the King's men were about to snatch the university's property.

✤ King Henry VIII (1491–1547)

By now, Henry was a sick old man. The story went that Henry's sixth wife, Catherine Parr, was a friend to Cambridge University. Catherine artfully suggested that Henry fund a royal college there to educate leaders who stayed loyal to the Crown.

Besides, Henry was a sincere Christian and worried about the state of his soul. He founded Trinity College in 1546, the year before he died. He chose the name Trinity to honor the Christian teaching that three entities—God the Father, Jesus Christ the Son, and the Holy Spirit—are one and the same. Henry wanted to please God in this life before he passed on to the next.

✤ Trinity College, c. 1890 Library of Congress LC-DIG-ppmsc-08091

books in his old room at Mr. Clark's home while the servant did Isaac's work. One day, as Isaac returned home on horseback, he dismounted to lead the horse up a hill. Somehow the horse slipped out of its bridle. But Isaac never noticed. He continued on home, dragging the horseless bridle behind him. Indeed, Isaac was miserable at farming, and he was miserable while farming, too.

To Isaac's good fortune, two men in his life intervened with his mother. Hannah's brother, Isaac's uncle William Ayscough, and his schoolmaster, Mr. Stokes, visited Hannah to plead for Isaac to return to the King's School. Mr. Stokes even agreed to drop Isaac's fees in order to persuade Isaac's tightfisted mother to let him go back.

Both men agreed that Isaac was destined for more learning; a few more months of preparation, and Isaac would be ready to enter Cambridge University. Uncle William Ayscough had a particular college at Cambridge in mind: his nephew would enter Trinity College, the same Cambridge college he had attended.

Isaac returned to the Clark household in Grantham and moved back into his old room. Sometime during his years at the King's School, he supposedly fell into a romantic "attachment" with Mr. Clark's stepdaughter. Many years later, this same woman, now the elderly "Mrs. Vincent," spoke of the warm feelings she and Isaac had shared as young people, but she said that she married someone else after Isaac left for university. Isaac himself never left anything written about her.

Mr. Stokes taught Isaac everything he could to prepare Isaac for his entrance examinations for Trinity College. Soon the day came when Isaac left Lincolnshire for Cambridge, a city and its namesake university that lay 60 miles away. Stopping in Woolsthorpe, Isaac gathered a few possessions and said good-bye to his family. It was early summer, just when a young man was most needed on a sheep farm.

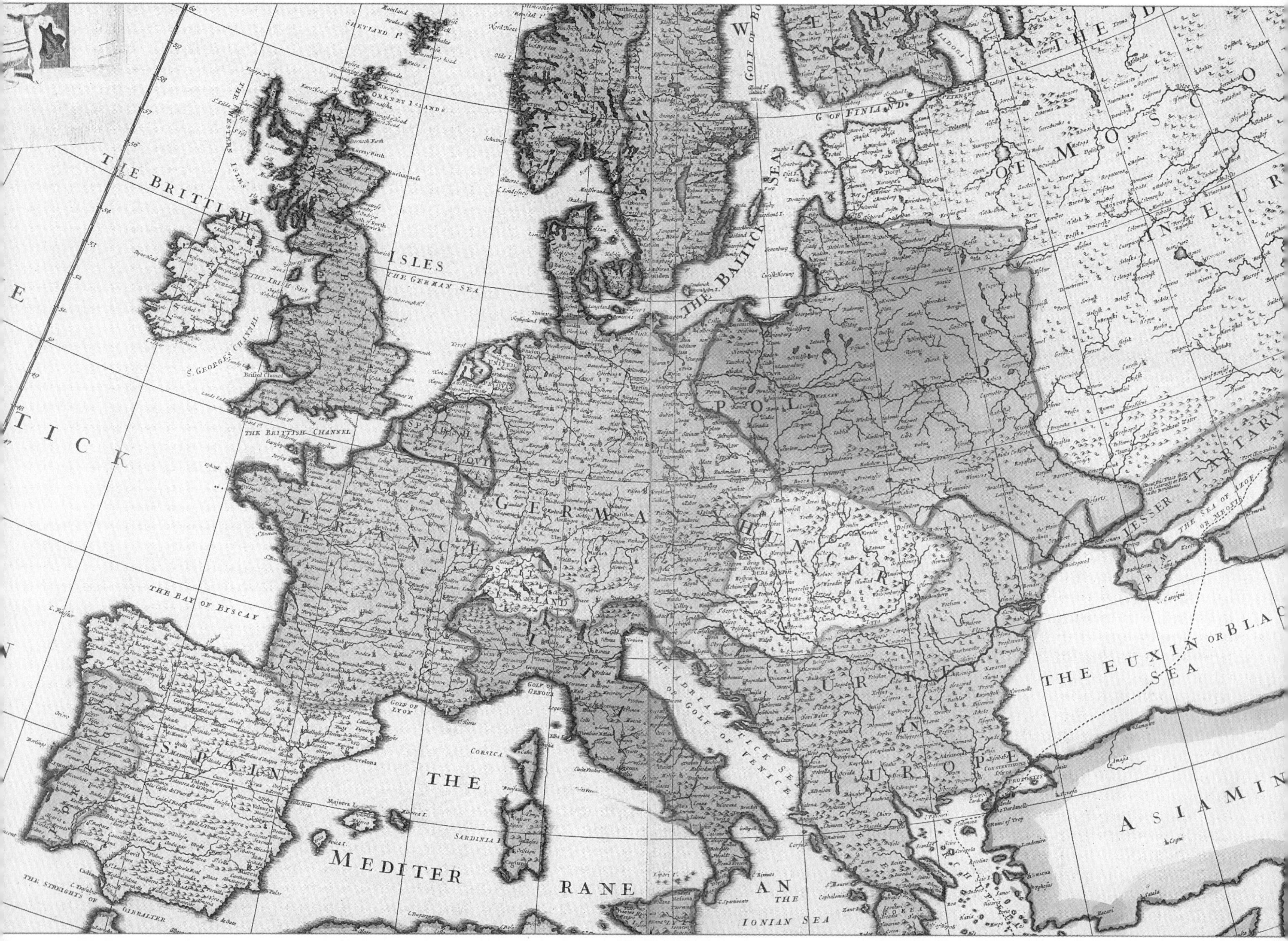
THE BRITTISH ISLES
THE GERMAN SEA
THE IRISH SEA
S.T GEORGES CHANNEL
THE BRITTISH CHANNEL
THE BALTICK SEA
GOLF OF FINIAND
GOLF OF BOTHNIA
POLAND
GERMANY
FRANCE
SPAIN
HUNGARY
TURKEY IN EUROPE
THE BAY OF BISCAY
THE MEDITERRANEAN
CORSICA
SARDINIA I.
GOLF OF LYON
GOLF OF GENOUA
THE ADRIATICK SEA OR GOLF OF VENICE
THE IONIAN SEA
THE EUXIN OR BLAC SEA
LESSER TARTARY
THE SEA OF AZOF OR MEOTIS
ASIA MIN
THE STREIGHTS OF GIBRALTER
SHETLAND I.S
ORKNEY ISLANDS
THE WESTERN ISLES
OF MOSCO
IN EUR

CHAPTER

STUDY AT CAMBRIDGE

WHAT A LONG, strange trip it was! The road to Cambridge, all 60 miles of it, stretched ahead of Isaac Newton. The ancient track, which dated back to times when Rome held a good part of England in its empire, now led to education and opportunities for Newton.

The road took the 18-year-old away from all he knew—his mother and half-siblings in tiny Woolsthorpe, and his school in the small village of Grantham. Onward he rode. The journey from Woolsthorpe to Cambridge took three days on horseback.

By the time Isaac Newton rode into town in June 1661, Cambridge straddled both sides of the River Cam. During the first century A.D., the Romans put a military fort at the site when they saw that Cambridge was a vital link on the road they'd built to move their soldiers from Colchester to Lincoln. A bridge constructed in the late 700s enabled Cambridge to grow from two small villages just across from each other to one thriving market town, an ideal location for river travelers to mix with traders who followed the old Roman road.

Lively and loud, Cambridge also was home to its namesake Cambridge University. Students and their masters (teachers) rubbed elbows with townspeople along Cambridge's rough paved streets. It was easy to tell the hometown people from the university folk. Both students and masters wore gowns and caps that signified their standing in school and to which of Cambridge University's colleges they belonged. Inside the university's walls, some of these colleges had existed since the late 1200s. Their names—Kings, Queens, Jesus, Trinity—

✤ A map of Europe printed about 1700.
Library of Congress G5700 17—.S4 TIL

illustrated the links that the university had to both the Crown in London and the Church of England.

Today Cambridge stands as one of the great universities of the world, but in 1661, its classes offered little to respect. In London, members of Parliament heard reports that young men in Europe were studying subjects like chemistry, anatomy, botany, mathematics, and history. But the subjects their own sons studied at Cambridge were not as advanced. It was only 30 miles across the English Channel, but new ideas from France, Germany, and Italy arrived late to Cambridge and were adopted slowly.

An Outdated Outlook on the Universe

As Isaac Newton began his studies at Cambridge, students were learning about the worldview of the early Greeks, especially Aristotle, the best known of the Greek thinkers. Aristotle lived in Athens from 384 to 322 B.C., during its prime, when the small city-state gave birth to Western civilization and Western knowledge. Aristotle's ideas dominated the thinking of scholars for two thousand years after his death, right up until the mid-1600s, when Isaac and others at Cambridge studied about him.

✤ A view of early Cambridge from the west.

By reading their masterworks, Newton learned that the Greeks looked for perfection in the universe. They believed that simple things were the most beautiful, and this ideal underscored their civilization. For instance, Newton quickly grasped that Greek architecture was based on the ideals of Greek mathematics, which emphasized straight lines, perfect circles, and simple geometric shapes such as squares and triangles.

Newton continued to learn more about Aristotle's worldview. The Greek philosopher pictured the universe divided into two separate parts: one, the earth and its moon; the other, everything beyond. In the earthbound or "terrestrial" region, Aristotle wrote, everything is made up of four elements—earth, water, air, and fire. Within the earth–moon system, imperfection and change are expected, as when the moon changes its face every night.

However, Aristotle imagined a totally different situation beyond the moon. Out there stretches a perfect place called the celestial region, what we call "outer space." All things move in exact circles, always in good order, everything perfect, and nothing changing, ever.

Aristotle claimed that the sun and planets orbit the earth in perfect circles, too. During the Middle Ages, Catholic monks who adapted Aristotle's ideas to Roman Catholic teachings agreed with him. The sun and the five planets—the only planets they knew about at the time—orbited the earth, each in its own crystal sphere. Layer by layer, each sphere enveloped the next one in a multilayered universe.

Aristotle also believed in a God that directs the universe and keeps everything in constant motion. He went on to say that this Supreme Being does not rely on anything else to make it move. It simply "is." Aristotle thought of this Supreme Being as the "Unmoved Mover" of all things.

❖ The ancient Greeks based their architecture on the ideals of geometry. The U.S. Capitol Building is a more recent example of classic Greek architecture based on simple geometric shapes. Architect of the Capitol

A medieval artist's idea of Aristotle at work.
Library of Congress LC-USZ62-110306

Aristotle's ideas about God also appealed to Catholic scholars during the Middle Ages. Aristotle's belief in a Supreme Being connected nicely to the Christian belief in one God who has no beginning and no end. Christian leaders also agreed with Aristotle's claim that Earth—and the people whom God created to have power over the earth—stands in the very middle of all creation. This idea is known as the geocentric, or "Earth-centered," universe.

In 1600, hundreds of years after the Middle Ages, some Cambridge teachers still assumed that Aristotle's worldview was correct. Certainly it made sense. They saw the sun rise and set day in and day out. Every 28 days, the moon passed through its phases, starting as a small sliver, waxing each night until full, then waning until its face hid in darkness, only to appear once more. With their own eyes, they could track Mars and Venus as wandering back and forth against the background of stars; the word *planet* actually means "wanderer."

If an earth-centered view was good enough for the highly-respected Aristotle, it was good enough for most folk in Cambridge. But as Isaac Newton arrived at Cambridge in 1661, astronomers on the European continent were turning learning upside down. Aristotle's concept of an earth-centered universe began to wither away.

Astronomers Undo Aristotle

Aristotle's geocentric model puzzled some astronomers. In 1514 a Polish priest, Nicolaus Copernicus, declared that Aristotle and the Catholic Church were wrong. The sun—not the earth—stands in the center of the universe. This we call the heliocentric, or sun-centered, system. Although he could not prove it, Copernicus was on to a big idea.

In the late 1500s, a wealthy Danish astronomer, Tycho Brahe, had the best-equipped observatory in Europe. He recorded vast amounts of data about the positions of planets and stars. In November 1572, Tycho discovered a supernova (an exploding star), proving that it lay far beyond the moon, where everything was supposedly pure and unchanging. According to the Church Fathers, this couldn't happen. Tycho suggested that planets circle the sun as the entire group circles the earth. Tycho named this plan the Tychonic System.

In 1600 a young mathematician, Johannes Kepler, visited Tycho at work for the Holy Roman Emperor in Czechoslovakia. Tycho kept excellent records, but he never could describe the grand design of stars and constellations in a mathematical way. Tycho wanted Kepler to work out the formula. But

PHASES OF THE MOON

YOU MIGHT THINK that the moon goes through its phases because the earth is casting a shadow on it. Not true! Phases of the moon depend on where the earth and moon stand in relation to the sun, and each other. The moon goes through its phases every 28/29 days in what we call the "lunar cycle." (*Lunar* refers to the moon and has its roots in Latin.) Here's how to see the lunar cycle for yourself.

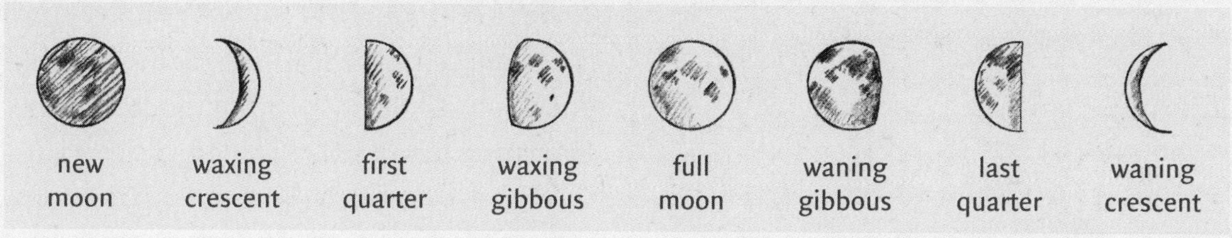

YOU'LL NEED

- Floor lamp or table lamp
- Thin stick, such as a chopstick or pencil
- Six-inch foam ball
- Darkened room

Remove the lampshade from the lamp and place it in an open area of the room. You need enough room to turn around with your arm extended.

Poke the stick into the foam ball. This is your model of the moon. The lamp is the sun and your head is the earth.

Turn out the lights in the room, leaving only the lamp on.

Hold the ball in your right hand at arm's length between you and a little way above the light. You will see that the surface of the ball is dark. We call this phase the *new moon* or the *dark of the moon*.

Turn slowly to the left and watch as a fingernail of light appears on the surface of the ball. This is the waxing crescent moon. *Waxing* means "growing."

Continue to turn to the left until the moon is half lit—the first quarter moon. How far have you turned from your "sun?" As you continue your journey, the moon grows into a waxing gibbous moon. *Gibbous* is a term used to describe being bigger than half but less than a full moon.

When your back is to the sun, what has happened to the moon? (It should be fully illuminated.) You are looking at the full moon. You are now halfway through the lunar cycle.

Continue your slow, leftward rotation through the rest of the lunar cycle. Your model moon will go through its waning (shrinking) gibbous phase to its third quarter.

Finally, the moon cycles through its waning crescent phase until once again you are facing the light.

Ask yourself: How would you hold your model moon to show a lunar eclipse?

THINKING AHEAD

You might want to track the phases of the moon. The moonrise takes place about every 25 hours, and you can usually find out the exact moonrise time during a weather broadcast. Obviously, sometimes you can't see the moonrise because you're sound asleep. Other times, the moon rises and crosses the sky during daytime, when sunlight hides it. However, you can still track the moon by making notes in your Waste Book every day for a month or two.

Kepler had his own ideas; he planned to use Tycho's data to map a new concept of the universe.

When Tycho died in 1601, Kepler replaced him. Like others, Kepler envisioned planets orbiting in perfect circles, so Kepler searched Tycho's notes about Mars's orbit. Instead of fitting Tycho's data into the concept of a circular orbit, Kepler studied the facts for what the *numbers* told him. He discovered that Mars travels in a slightly flattened orbit called an ellipse—an oval.

Kepler published his astonishing breakthrough in 1609. Most astronomers ignored him; the idea of planets traveling in anything but perfect circles was unthinkable.

Galileo the Great

GALILEO Galilei (1564–1642) was a professor of mathematics at the University of Padua in the republic of Venice, in Italy, from 1592 to 1610. Like other natural philosophers, he taught about all kinds of things besides math, including engineering and astronomy. His low pay reflected the low status that mathematics and natural philosophy had in Padua at the time.

✤ Nicolaus Copernicus (1473–1543)

✤ Tycho Brahe (1546–1601)

✤ Johannes Kepler (1571–1630)

In 1608 Galileo learned about a new "plaything" invented in Holland: the telescope. Galileo was a genius, and he quickly grasped what such an instrument could do for the research that he loved. Using the high quality glass that was made in Venice, Galileo ground lenses and inserted them into a tube. Now he held a telescope that magnified faraway objects to appear eight times larger. He then built even better telescopes, instruments with 20- and 30-power magnification.

Galileo trained his telescopes toward the moon. It took some time for him to interpret what he saw as he watched shadows change on the lunar surface. But once he understood what he was looking at, Galileo knew he had made a giant discovery. The moon was not the perfect object Aristotle had envisioned. Its surface was rough with the same kinds of features that appeared on Earth, tall mountains and huge craters that pockmarked everything. When Galileo turned his telescope toward Jupiter, he viewed not only the immense, colorful planet but four wonderful surprises, Jupiter's moons.

In 1610 Galileo published his discoveries in a short pamphlet he entitled *Sidereus nuncius* (*Starry Messenger*). Craftily, he named Jupiter's four moons the "Medicean stars" and sent his little book to the powerful Medici (MED-uh-chee) family who ruled the city-state of Florence, Italy. As Galileo had hoped, an invitation soon arrived from the Grand Duke Cosimo II de'Medici. Soon Galileo took his place as chief mathematician and philosopher at the glittering court of the powerful Medici family.

✤ Galileo shows a telescope to a group of Italian ladies. Library of Congress LC-USZ62-110447

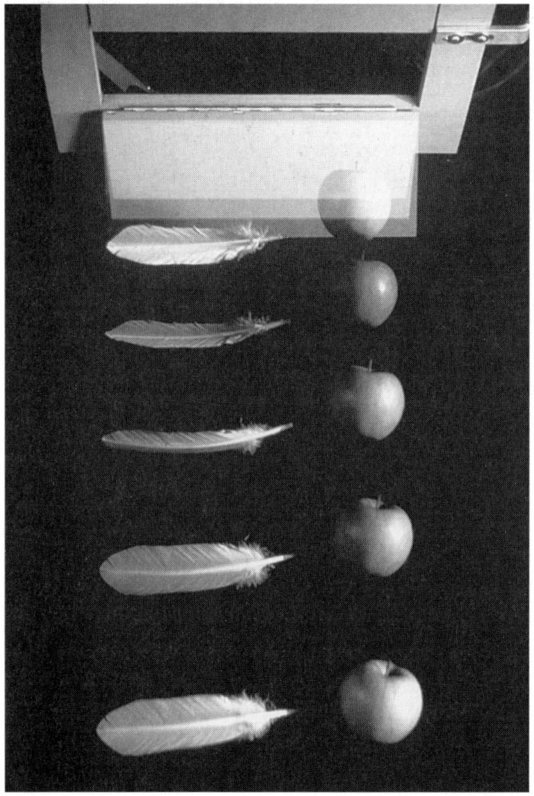

✤ In a vacuum chamber where there is no air, an apple and a feather fall at exactly the same rate of speed.

©Jim Sugar

The name "Florence" refers to the Latin word *flora*, meaning "flower." Indeed the flower of Italian cities, Florence stood at the heart of the Renaissance. Here, the Medici Court sparkled with learning. The Medicis led the pack of European royalty who filled their households with experts in all of the exciting subjects studied during the Renaissance. Their courtiers were engineers, mapmakers, astronomers, surgeons, and artists. No longer were Catholic monasteries the center of education. Europe's royal families paid salaries to their courtiers and thus became the sponsors of new learning.

Galileo grew up with Aristotle's belief that objects fall at a speed in proportion to their weight. In other words, the heavier an object is, the faster it will fall. This idea appeared to make sense; a roof tile falling off a building seemingly hits the ground faster than does a wooden shingle. But after giving the issue lots of thought, Galileo arrived at a far different conclusion. He theorized that in a vacuum, where there is no air to resist them, all objects would fall at the exact same rate of speed. The roof tile and the shingle would hit the ground at exactly the same time. Galileo called this the "law of falling bodies." Galileo went on to say that, here on Earth, air resists falling objects. Therefore, the longer an object travels, the faster it will fall, up to a limit known as "terminal velocity."

Supposedly, Galileo tested his new ideas by climbing the Leaning Tower of Pisa to drop lead balls off the top. This might very well be a tale that made for a good story, but Galileo did roll different sizes of bronze balls down long, smooth, inclined planes to test the concept, and he had the same result. The balls' speed increased in proportion to the amount of time that elapsed, but *not* in proportion to their masses.

Then Galileo turned to the question of projectiles, things like arrows, spears, cannonballs, and rockets. First, he said, they follow the Law of Falling Bodies, always returning to Earth after being thrown or launched. Next, he theorized that they stayed in flight because of their inertia. Inertia is the tendency of things to stay in motion unless something else stops them.

This notion of inertia directly opposed Aristotle's worldview. Aristotle said that every moving object moved because something *else* was making it move. But Aristotle was wrong, Galileo said. Inertia just happens, just *is*; once a projectile is airborne, nothing else pushes it along. Again, Galileo was striking out at old ideas as he made his way to new ones.

Now well paid and highly regarded by powerful people in Florence, Galileo prospered. He let everyone know that he agreed with Copernicus's outrageous idea. His observations confirmed it. The earth orbited the sun. The earth, Galileo declared, was just a planet like all the others.

This pronouncement got Galileo into trouble with the other power player in Italy, the Roman Catholic Church. The Church taught that God had placed human beings on Earth in the very center of creation. A special court of the Catholic Church called the "Inquisition" charged Galileo with the crime of heresy—that is, Galileo's ideas went against the Church's official beliefs. Galileo faced being burned at the stake. There was no way out if the Church court condemned him as a heretic, or non-believer.

Galileo traveled to Rome to face his accusers in a religious trial. By now, he was an old man, and he confessed to his "crime" even though he knew the truth. Galileo spent the rest of his days under house arrest. Seventy years old and partly blind, he kept at his research and produced another amazing book, *Discorsi e dimostrazioni matematiche, intorno a due nuove scienze (Discourses on Two New Sciences).*

In his new book, Galileo wrote about the strength of common materials like wood and marble, the properties of liquids, the weight of air, and how pendulums swing. In the book's second half, Galileo went on to talk about the nature of motion. However, Galileo's thinking never went far enough to actually arrive at the concept of gravity. That milestone would fall to another natural philosopher: Isaac Newton.

Galileo Galilei died in 1642. Newton was born less than a year later.

✤ Galileo, whose discoveries went against the teachings of the Roman Catholic Church, was forced to appear before the Inquisition. Library of Congress LC-USZ62-11047

WATCH A PENDULUM SWING

AS GALILEO WATCHED a large hanging lamp swing from the ceiling of a church, he noticed how it always took the same amount of time to swing back and forth, just like a pendulum that swings beneath a clock. A pendulum's "period," one complete swing, does change with its length but not its weight. An ideal pendulum, no matter how heavy, always swings an equal distance in the same amount of time.

You can test Galileo's idea for yourself.

YOU'LL NEED

- Scissors
- Kite string, fishing line, or thin, stiff twine
- Paper clip
- Different kinds of weights (washers and fishing weights work well)
- Tape
- Helper (to time your experiment)
- Watch or clock with a second hand

1. Cut a piece of string 30 inches long and tie a paper clip to one end. Attach a washer to the paper clip.

2. Tape the end of the string to the edge of a table or countertop so that the weight can swing freely.

3. Pull back the hanging weight from the table, keeping the string straight, until it is parallel to the floor. When your helper says "Go," release the weight and let the pendulum swing freely. Count how many times the pendulum swings back and forth in 15 seconds. (One swing is complete when the pendulum has gone back and forth once and returns to its starting point.)

4. Repeat the process a few times. Record your observations in your Waste Book on a table similar to the one below.

5. Now hold the weight at a 45-degree angle to the table leg—half as high as the first time. Ask yourself "How many times will the pendulum swing in 15 seconds?" Then let the pendulum go. Are you surprised at the result?

6. Add more weight to the same piece of string and repeat the experiment. What do you expect will happen? What is your result?

7. Now shorten the string to be 15 inches long. Repeat both parts of your experiment. Which length string—15 or 30 inches—produces the greatest number of swings per minute? The fewest? What could explain any differences among your results?

MY EXPERIMENT: Watch a Pendulum Swing **TODAY'S DATE** ________

PENDULUM DATA CHART

Length of String	Type of Weight	Parallel or 45° Angle	Number of Swings in 15 seconds (one complete back-and-forth motion)

NOTES: ________________________________

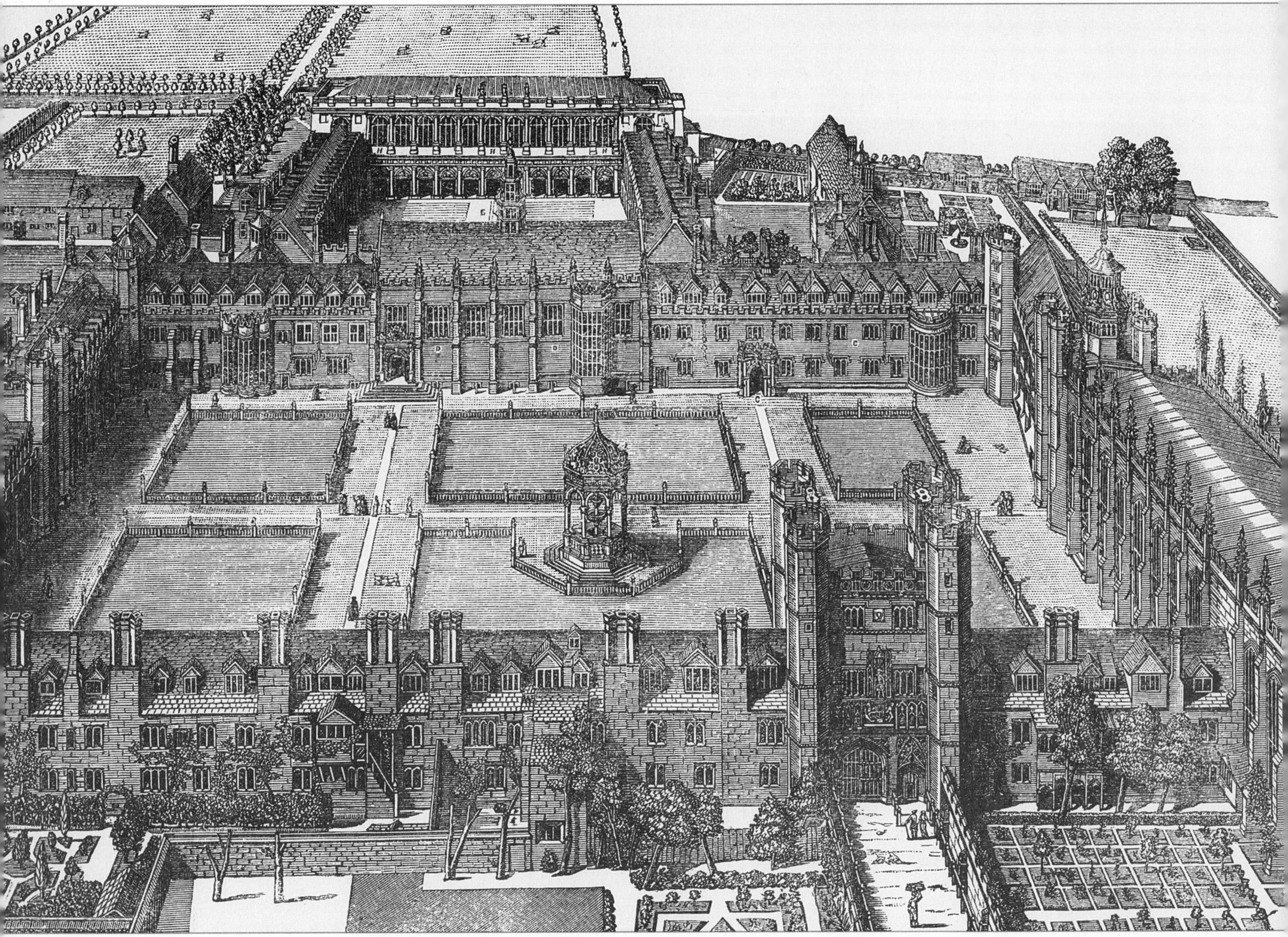

CHAPTER 3

NEWTON THE MISFIT

HANNAH NEWTON SENT Isaac to Cambridge with only a small amount of money for her son's education. Thanks to her inheritance from Newton's stepfather, which added to income from her farm in Woolsthorpe, Hannah Newton Smith was a wealthy woman. But she was not willing to share her wealth with her son, at least not for a university education.

Hannah wanted to keep her son in farming. She had insisted on paying reduced fees when Isaac returned to school in Grantham. When Isaac entered Cambridge University, her mind didn't change. Hannah packed Isaac off to college with just a few coins in his pockets when she could have afforded to set him up in style. Isaac only had enough for necessities. He wrote in his notebook that he spent some of his money for things like candles, ink, an ink bottle, and a chamber pot (apparently students brought their own toileting receptacles to keep under their beds).

By her actions, Hannah made it clear that if Isaac truly desired to go to university, he would have to work his way through. Thus, Isaac entered Trinity College in a most humiliating fashion: as a sizar.

Sizars worked as servants to Trinity's teachers or well-off students. Probably the young sizar was not on a first-name basis with those he served. Isaac became known at Cambridge simply as "Newton."

Newton stood on the bottom rung of the social ladder, a rigid system that reflected life at Trinity College, Cambridge University, and all of England itself. In the mid-1600s, Trinity's students split into roughly three groups that were examples

of the way English society divided itself by class. At the top stood the wealthy students, called gentlemen fellows. They were sons of wealthy fathers who bought their sons' way into Cambridge. These young men got credit for work even when they skipped classes, were allowed to eat dinner with their professors, and got away with all kinds of mischief—not to mention some serious wrongdoing.

✤ (LEFT) The Trinity College emblem. (BELOW) An engraving of Trinity College as it appeared in Isaac Newton's day.

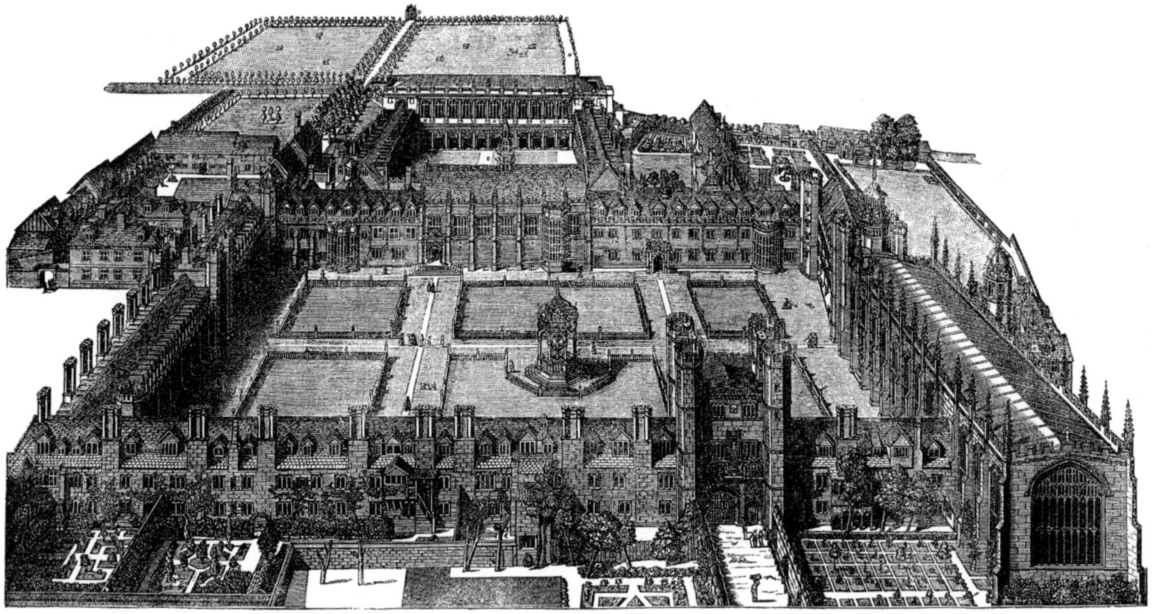

In the middle group of students stood the pensioners—sons of small businessmen and lower clergy who paid part of their own expenses to attend university. Upper class students still thought of pensioners as poor because pensioners lacked the high social standing of the students who ranked above them. Sometimes, however, the father of a pensioner might purchase a spot for his oldest son to sit with the richer students. At that point the first-born son became a gentleman fellow who could buy his way into the upper ranks of students.

At the bottom of this social pile were the sizars. They were the poorest students, whose fathers owned small farms or served as clergy in unimportant churches. These students had to work at Trinity to pay for their education as well their food and lodgings. The sizars were known for working hard at their studies.

In return for his work as a sizar, Newton was allowed to attend lectures, study with a tutor, and share a room for sleep and studying. However, he was closed out of the more interesting events. When important visitors made speeches at Trinity College, only the masters and wealthy gentlemen fellows could attend. By today's standards, such a system might seem unfair, but, as people in all walks of life know very well, money "talks." Wealth and social standing were two sides of the same coin, and rank certainly had its privileges at Cambridge University.

Morning chores must have come as a shock to Newton, who was used to having servants of his own at home in Woolsthorpe. Now he had to rise early, dress, and make his way to the kitchen to gulp down a cold breakfast of bread and beer before he took meals upstairs to the rooms of people he served. He also had the nasty task of gathering chamber pots from their rooms to empty them. In the evening, he again served meals to the higher class students in Trinity College's Great Hall. Only after his final chore could he and the other sizars dine on the leftovers.

Still, Isaac Newton lived in a style that was a cut above the rest of the sizars at Trinity. His notebooks reflected his social life outside of school. The entries he wrote showed that he had just enough extra money to make loans to both his fellow sizars and the pensioner students who supposedly outranked him. He recorded their names in his notebook, and when a loan was repaid, he crossed their names out. Perhaps Newton was doing favors for the pensioners so that he could become friends with them; Newton no doubt felt he belonged with their group instead of with the other sizars. He

❖ Under King Henry VIII's gaze, Isaac Newton waited on higher-ranking students in the Great Hall at Trinity College.

Water Clock or Candle Clock?

ACCURATE MECHANICAL CLOCKS with pendulums did not arrive on the scene until the middle of the 1600s. During Isaac Newton's childhood, his neighbors looked at the sun's position to gauge the time or used hourglasses to measure shorter periods. For thousands of years, water clocks, burning ropes, and candle clocks all helped people keep track of time.

You can make a candle clock and a simple water clock to find out just how useful these clocks were to people in earlier days.

Make a Candle Clock

Adult supervision required

YOU'LL NEED

- Several same-sized 3-inch birthday candles
- Piece of clay
- Matches
- Ruler
- Thin permanent marker

Place two candles in a piece of clay. If your candles are pointed, burn them just enough to make them flat on top, then blow them out. Make sure that the tops of your candles are the same height.

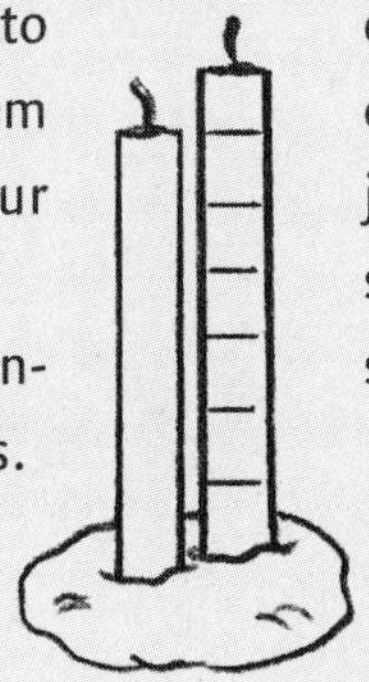

Have an adult helper light one candle and let it burn for five minutes. Blow it out. Use a ruler to measure how far down the first candle burned. Use this number to help you measure and draw several five-minute marks on the second candle. This will be your candle clock. Set it aside.

Make a Water Clock

YOU'LL NEED

- Large pushpin, tack, or small nail
- Disposable plastic cup (the kind that will bend if you squeeze it)
- Clear jar with straight sides and an opening large enough to support the paper cup
- Water
- Thin permanent marker
- Ruler
- Measuring cup
- Watch with a second hand or a digital timer

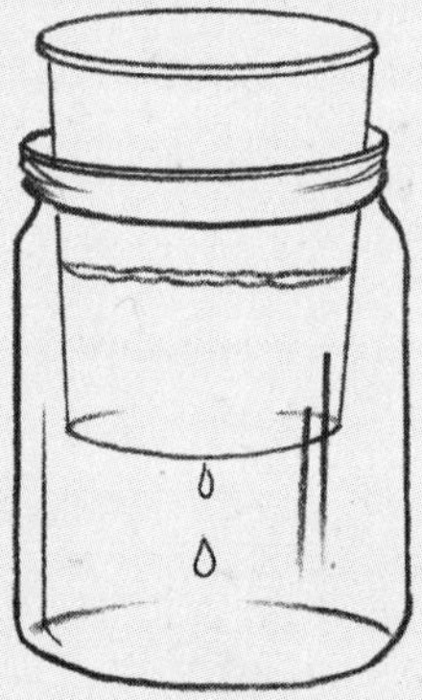

Use a pushpin to make a small hole in the bottom of a disposable plastic cup. Place the cup in the jar so that it is suspended above the bottom, as shown. Now pour in about ½ cup water. Has it started to drip? You might need to tap the cup to get it started.

Once there's a steady drip, mark the water level in the jar after five minutes have passed. (It's OK to add more water to the cup if you need to.) Then, empty out your water clock. Use a ruler to measure how far up the jar the water reached. Use this measurement to help you draw several five-minute marks on the jar. This will be your water clock. Set it aside.

Compare Clocks

Now set your candle clock alongside the water clock. Fill the plastic cup while keeping the hole plugged with your finger. As your adult helper lights the candle, set the cup in the jar and allow it to drip.

Watch both of your clocks for five minutes. What do you observe? Which clock is more accurate? Can you use one of your clocks to time something you do that takes just a few minutes, like making your bed or brushing and flossing your teeth?

Think of something to do that takes about 30 minutes, like baking a pan of brownies. How could you use what you learned to design a longer-running candle clock or water clock?

also joined students who gathered in taverns around Cambridge. Newton's notes showed that he both won and lost bets when he played cards, though Newton claimed that he never lost a game of "draughts"—what we call checkers.

Even so, as with the boys at school in Grantham, Newton did not fit in. Already he was a year or two older than his fellow students in Trinity College. He was no longer just the head boy at a small school. He was nearly grown up, and his thinking was maturing as well.

It soon became clear to Newton that he knew as much as or more about natural philosophy than even some of the masters. He could see for himself that he was gifted with a remarkable ability to solve difficult problems about vast numbers of subjects. Newton also saw that he knew more about mathematics than nearly everyone at Trinity College. Yet no one else realized it at the time.

During his early years at Cambridge, Newton never spoke outright about the thinking going on deep inside his head. As he filled his notebooks with ideas and experiments in all kinds of subjects, never did he share them with his teachers or other students. Newton took great care to hide his work.

As with all the others at Trinity College, Newton studied theology, the nature of God. In Newton's day, every learned person studied theology. In fact, it was the destiny of every professor at Trinity to take holy orders and become a priest in the Church of England; this was a rule. So Newton, too, moved beyond the study of the natural world to think about spiritual matters.

Again Newton departed from the usual thinking among members of the Church of England. Newton absolutely believed in God, but as the years wore on, Newton began to question some of the Church's basic teachings that others held to be sacred. Newton was very quiet about his differences and only began to share them with a few close friends when he was a much older man. Perhaps he feared that no one would believe what he had to say. Most likely, Newton was caught up in his work like a spider snared in her own web.

Like so many men and women with enormous intelligence, Newton didn't see things the way most people do. He locked onto problems and would not let go until he had considered them from every possible angle.

Students and teachers at Cambridge University picked up on Newton's odd ways. Then, as now, geniuses often act differently than others and do not relate to the group. We can only imagine that the other students and masters looked at him with a mix of curiosity and dislike.

CREATE OPTICAL ILLUSIONS

WHEN ISAAC NEWTON first attended Cambridge, he acted as his own guinea pig by staring into the sun to find out what would happen . . . and he nearly blinded himself. *No one should ever look at the sun.*

The way humans actually see something is called "perception." Isaac Newton also did experiments to correct a misperception that many people had when he was a boy. Their eyes told them that the sun circles the earth. Therefore, they believed that Earth was at the center of the universe.

Your eyes can also play tricks on you. In the first optical illusion, you will learn how both of your eyes work together to keep an image in focus. This ability is called "binocular vision." What kinds of misperceptions can you discover?

YOU'LL NEED

- Pencil

Make a pencil jump while holding it still. Start by holding the pencil at arm's length, perpendicular to the floor. Close one eye and line up the pencil so that it's parallel with a straight object in the background, such as a window or door frame.

While holding the pencil perfectly still, open the eye that was shut and shut the other eye. Then switch eyes back and forth rapidly. What do you see? What is really happening?

Try this optical illusion next. Can you see 11 fingers? Put the tips of your index fingers together and hold them about a foot away from your eyes.

Keep your eyes focused on your fingertips and slowly move your fingers closer to your eyes. Can you see an 11th finger appear between the two tips, with a fingernail on each end? (It looks a bit like a weird little sausage.) What's happening to your perception?

In this final illusion, you'll watch the bee land on the flower without bending the page. Hold this page a foot away, then move the page slowly toward your face while staring at the bee and flower. At some point the bee will "fly" to the flower when your eyes cannot focus on both objects at the same time.

A Fierce Friendship

Newton started at Cambridge during the opening days of the reign of King Charles II. In 1660 the English Parliament welcomed King Charles II to the throne following England's Civil War. The King and his courtiers restored glamour and style to London. Many of the London students brought their freewheeling style to Cambridge. University officials mostly looked the other way as a fair number of students skipped church services—which were required—and crowded into taverns and coffeehouses. Even worse, some kept company with women of questionable backgrounds when they knew they should socialize only with young ladies of good breeding.

Like college boys everywhere, the young men at Cambridge were a mix of serious and not-so-serious—some students destined to become priests of the Church of England and others, the "party animals" who were at the university for a good time. Then, as now, serious students did not make good roommates with the merrymakers. Clashes were bound to happen.

As ill luck would have it, Newton found himself sharing a chamber with a reveler for at least the first year-and-a-half of his student days. Then, by chance, he bumped into another Trinity student who was in the same predicament. Newton and the other student were taking a walk around the college grounds, probably trying to get away from noisy gatherings back in their rooms. That student was named John Wickins, a pensioner. Like Newton, Wickins took his studies very seriously.

In 1727, after both Wickins and Newton were dead, Wickins's son wrote a letter to explain how his father came to be Isaac Newton's roommate:

> *My Father's Intimacy with Him came by meer Accident My Fathers first Chamberfellow being very disagreeable to him he retired one day into the walks, where he found Mr Newton solitary & dejected; Upon entering into discourse they found their cause of Retirement the same, & thereupon agreed to shake off their present disorderly Companions & Chum together, which they did as soon as conveniently they could & so continued as long as My Father staid at College...*

Newton and Wickins "chummed" as roommates. From all appearances, John Wickins was Newton's only true friend at Cambridge University for his entire stay there. Newton was indeed lucky to make—and to keep—Wickins's friendship.

Wickins played a quiet but priceless role in becoming Newton's assistant as the work

✤ (ABOVE) King Charles II and his lady friends enjoyed lighthearted, often silly games like "Hunting the Moth." (LEFT) The imposing statue of King Henry VIII looked over Isaac Newton as he took his walks around the grounds of Trinity College.

LOCATE YOUR LATITUDE

HUNDREDS OF YEARS before satellites and GPS systems, sailors used instruments called sextants to help them locate their latitude—how far north they were from the equator. To help them, they relied on Polaris, the North Star. To the human eye, Polaris is a "fixed" star, always in the same position over the North Pole.

Sailors used sextants to measure the angle between their positions and Polaris. This angle told them their position relative to the equator. For instance, Honolulu, Hawaii, lies at 21° north of the Equator. London, England lies at 51° north.

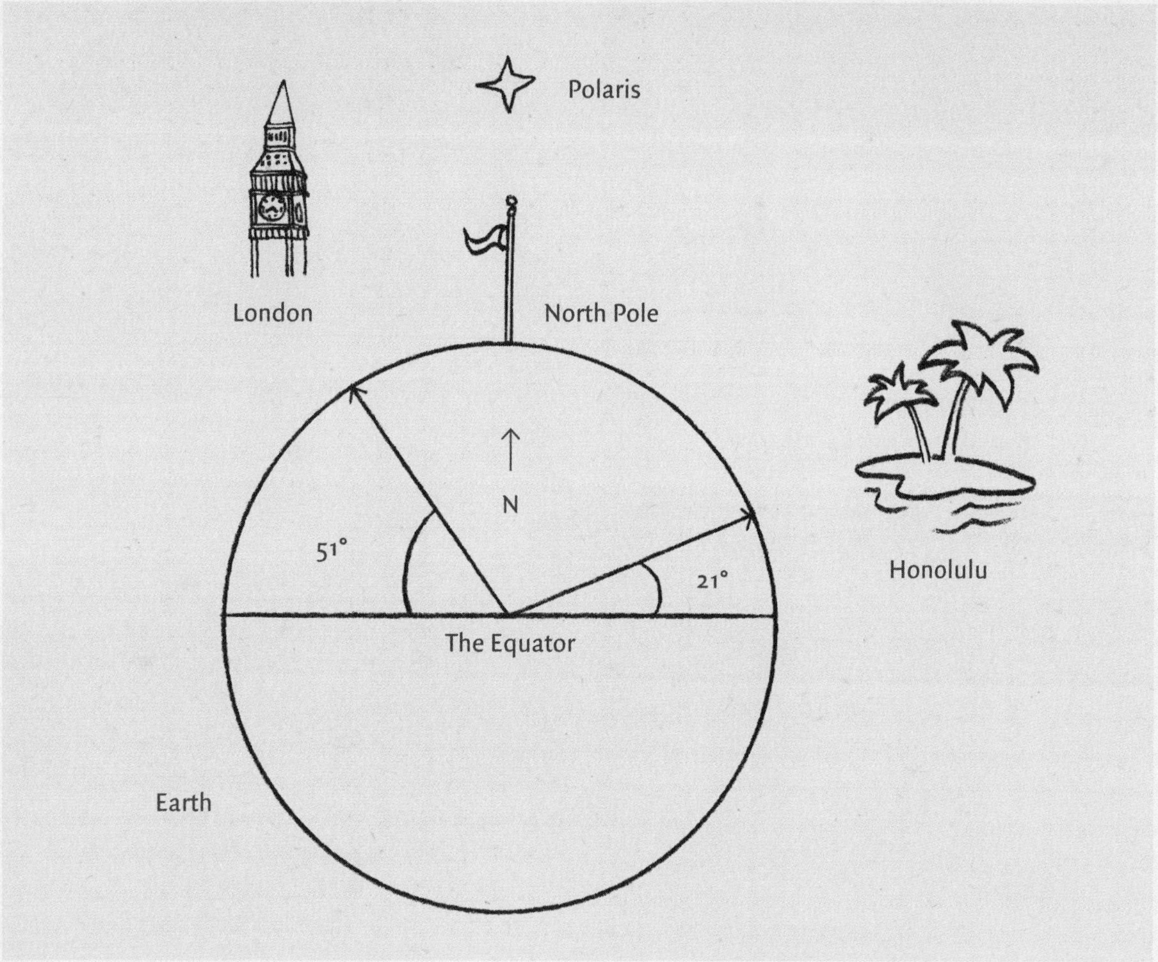

You can make a simple sextant and use it to find the latitude where you live. This experiment will work best on a clear, starry night.

YOU'LL NEED

- Pencil
- Tracing paper or a photocopy of the pattern at right
- 6-inch paper plate
- Scissors
- Glue
- Weight (such as a washer)
- 20-inch piece of fishing line or kite string
- Tape
- Drinking straw
- Partner
- Flashlight
- Waste Book
- Atlas or globe

1. Trace or photocopy the sextant pattern on the following page onto a sheet of paper. Glue the paper to the back of the paper plate, matching the curved edges. Cut out the pattern on the solid line. Cut a small slit along the solid line from the corner to the dot.

2. Tie the weight to one end of the fishing line. Knot the other end and thread it through the slit in your sextant.

3. Now tape the straw along the top edge of the sextant pattern as in the diagram. Do not tape over the string.

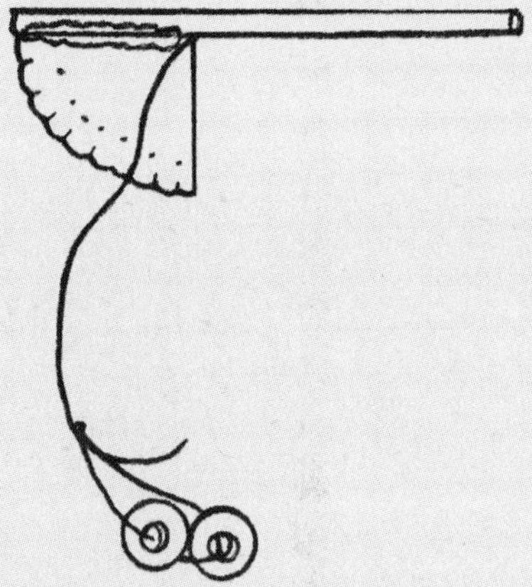

4. Go outside on a clear night and find "Polaris," the North Star. If you don't know where it is, look north for the constellations Ursa Major (the Great Bear, also called the "Big Dipper") and Ursa Minor (the Small Bear, also known as the "Little Dipper"). The North Star is the star on the very end of the handle on the constellation Ursa Minor. Still can't find it? Here's another hint: the two stars on the front, outside edge of the Big Dipper "point" to the North Star on Ursa Minor. You can find a star chart online at www.space.com/nightsky.

5. Close one eye. Let the weight hang freely on the string. Line up the straw between your open eye and Polaris so that you create a "sight line" between them. It's much easier to find Polaris by looking along the top of the straw instead of through it. Once you sight Polaris, have your partner use a flashlight and check where the string falls across the curved side. At what degree on your sextant does the string cross? This number is your latitude.

6. Check your results on the atlas or globe. Is your sextant accurate?

7. You can draw a picture of this activity in your Waste Book. Be sure to include the horizon, the North Star, and the spot where you are standing.

THINK: What would happen if you lived in the *Southern* Hemisphere, south of the equator? How would you find your latitude then?

SEXTANT PATTERN

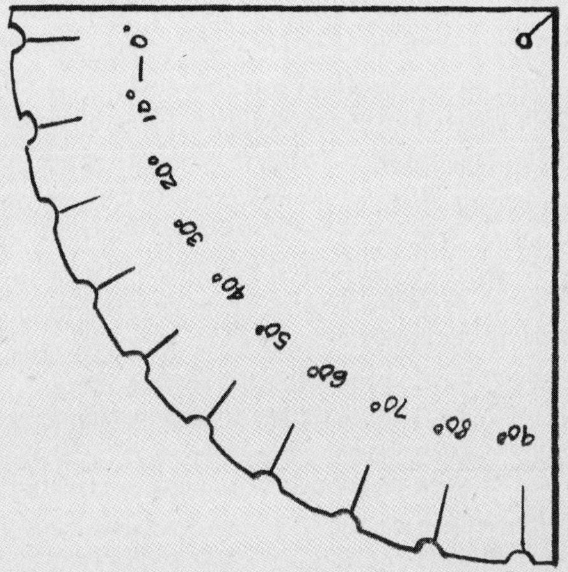

Comets

Comets are balls of grit and ice nearly as old as the solar system itself. Only in the mid-1900s did astronomers learn what comprises the nucleus of a comet. Sometimes described as "dirty snowballs," comets are roughly 25 percent dust and 75 percent ice, with a good measure of ammonia, methane, and carbon dioxide. Satellite photos in the 1980s confirmed that comets are so dirty with dust particles, they are practically black.

Comet Halley is a short-period comet appearing once in a human lifetime, about every 76 years. Ancient writings tell of comets that will not reappear for hundreds or thousands of years.

Comet Halley's tail shines brightly, but not all comets have tails. A comet must be constructed so that gases and bits of rocky material can escape through vents in its nucleus. As a comet approaches a star like our sun, solar radiation and solar wind cause the ice to sublime in long streams—go straight from a solid to a gas. A comet's tail always "blows" away from the sun.

Many comets experience "birth" in the Oort Cloud, a cold, giant cloud of particles that astronomers suspect hangs outside our solar system. Astronomers believe that every so often, gravity from a passing star kicks a comet out of the Oort Cloud into the sun's gravitational field. Other comets are thought to originate in the Kuiper Belt, a loose collection of dwarf planets (like Pluto) that encircle the solar system beyond Neptune.

Comets are born, and comets die. With every pass around the sun, a tiny piece of a comet vaporizes. But not to worry—30 new comets appear every year, destined to sweep by the earth for millions of years to come.

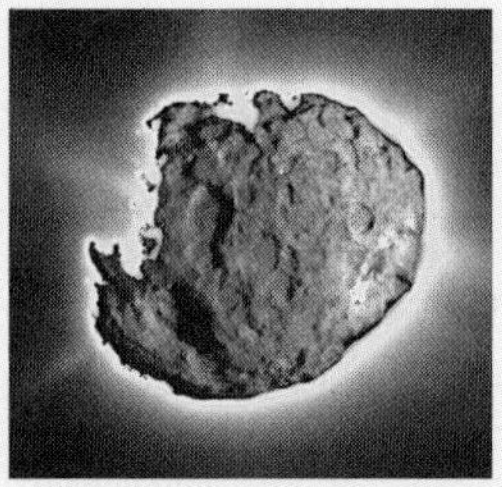

❖ (LEFT) Isaac Newton sketched pictures of the comet that swept across the Cambridge skies at Christmastime in 1664. Indiana University Library
(RIGHT) Comet Wild, a tailless comet. NASA

of his brilliant roommate unfolded over the next two decades. Doubtless, Wickins propped up both Newton's spirits and his actual health when Newton got tired or forgot to eat, which happened often. Their friendship was intense, and evidence hints that Newton guarded it with the jealousy of a madman.

The friendship ended abruptly in 1683 when Wickins, then a middle-aged man, decided to take a wife. He left Cambridge to marry, became a clergyman in a village parish, and raised a family. Newton seemingly took his friend's decision as a personal insult. There is no record that he ever spoke or wrote a letter to Wickins again.

Nonetheless, it seems that Newton did not forget his friend. When both were aging men, Newton sent a gift of a group of Bibles to Wickins so that his old chamber-fellow could use them in his parish.

CHAPTER 4

ASKING QUESTIONS

Like other new students at Trinity College, Newton met with a tutor during his early years at university. His name was Benjamin Pulleyn, a scholar who was well versed in many subjects. Newton made a point of reading through every assignment before he and Pulleyn discussed it. Frequently Newton knew as much as or more than his tutor did.

Apparently impressed, Pulleyn left his gifted student alone to study whatever he wished. Cambridge buzzed with talk about the work of a modern Frenchman named Rene Descartes (day-KART), the most famous philosopher of the day, and Newton decided that Descartes was a worthy subject. Descartes had an enormous intellect. His interests spanned the entire realm of knowledge in the first half of the 1600s. He studied natural philosophy and mathematics. He created a map of the universe, with Earth located in the middle of it. He answered questions about the nature of being a human when he stated, "I think, therefore I am." He asked about the nature of God, as well.

Descartes' work influenced teachers in universities all across Europe, who welcomed his up-to-date approach to learning. Descartes suggested that the universe works in a mechanical way. Planets, he wrote, move in currents of particles called vortices. Descartes' vortex theory accounted for his belief that there was no such thing as empty space. Something had to fill everything.

Newton tuned in to the talk about Descartes. Students could not enter Trinity's library unless accompanied by a teacher, but somehow Newton got his hands on Descartes' books and read them.

✽ Rene Descartes (1596–1650) Library of Congress LC-USZ62-61365

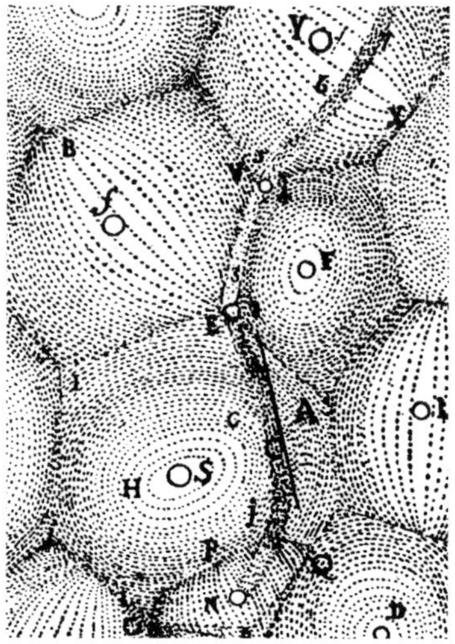

✽ Descartes' concept of planets traveling in vortices.

Descartes led Newton's thinking in many directions, first one way, and then another. Newton had about one hundred empty pages in the middle of a notebook. He filled a few of them with his thoughts on Descartes. Then he made an abrupt change. He made a list of everything he wanted to study.

Newton penned the words *Quaestiones quaedam philosophicae (Philosophical Questions).* He used the rest of his notebook to set up headings under which he outlined the rest of his plan for reading. By the time he was finished, 45 different topics were in the notebook. These topics spanned all the subjects in the field now known as physics, and much more:

> *Of Attomes. Of a Vacuum & Attomes. Of Quantity. Conjunction of bodys. Of Place. Of time & Eternity. The representation of a clock to goe by water or sand. Of Motion. Of the Celestiall matter & orbes. Of the Sunn Stars & Plannets & Comets. Of Rarity & Density. Rarefaction & Condensation. Of heate & cold. Of Gravity & Levity. Of violent Motion. Of Aer. Of Water & Salt. Of Earth. Of God. Of ye Creation. Of ye soule.*

The list goes on and on.

Newton's *Quaestiones* represent a threshold in human thinking. When Newton asked questions about the world around him, he also established the need to *answer* them. Did Isaac Newton know he was among the first to suggest that natural philosophers could perform experiments to answer their questions about science?

Newton began asking his *Quaestiones* sometime around 1662. In 1664 he moved on because different interests began to intrigue him. Descartes led him in a new direction, to the realm of mathematics.

A Genius Takes on Math

Newton arrived in Cambridge seemingly unprepared to tackle the algebra and geometry lessons that other students worked on with their tutors. The study of algebra had arrived at Cambridge by way of Latin translations from Islamic scholars, especially the work of an Arab mathematician named Al-Khwarizmi (al-kwar-IZ-mee), who lived from 780 to 850. Al-Khwarizmi's book, *al-jabr w' al-muqabalah*, gave us the word *algebra*. Algebra uses symbols like x, y, and z that make complex math problems easier to solve.

Geometry, however, was the invention of the early Greeks. Euclid, a mathematician who lived in Alexandria, Egypt, sometime around 300 B.C., organized the work of other Greek math scholars into a usable form. Euclid's geometry dealt with straight lines and shapes—triangles, squares, and circles—in two dimensions.

Both regular algebra and geometry bored Newton so quickly that he skipped right over them to tackle a different kind of problem. At this point, reading Descartes' books led Newton down a different path, this time to advanced mathematics. Descartes had written on a new form of math that took Euclid's geometry further than anyone had before. The French philosopher wanted to work out geometry problems in not two, but three dimensions—in real space, not just on paper. In order to reach his goal, Descartes applied algebra to geometry and called his new mathematics "analytical geometry."

Newton taught himself Descartes' new book, *La Géométrie* (*Geometry*); he didn't know anyone at Cambridge who could instruct him. Only a Latin version was available to him because Newton couldn't read French. He studied a few pages at a time, going over and over them until their meaning was clear. Then he moved on.

However, there lived in Trinity College someone who did understand Descartes' analytical geometry. To Newton's good fortune, Trinity College was the workplace of Dr. Isaac Barrow, by all accounts a brilliant scholar in subjects ranging from Greek to astronomy. Barrow belonged to the Royal Society, a distinguished group of gentlemen who met in London to discuss natural philosophy. Barrow's latest study had taken him into the realm of numbers, and he became Trinity College's first Lucasian Professor of Mathematics. Henry Lucas, a rich Englishman, had left money in his will so that Cambridge University could afford to pay a top mathematician. (Other famous names were to follow Barrow's as Lucasian Professor: Isaac Newton; astronomer George Airy; Charles Babbage, a mathematician who visualized the basics of computer programming; and Stephen Hawking, an acclaimed 21st-century physicist.)

But first Newton dealt with the same challenge as other Trinity students. In the spring of 1664, he had to pass a scholarship exam at Cambridge in order to win a permanent place there. Otherwise he would have to return to Woolsthorpe. The pressure was on.

Newton faced tough competition: a large group of young men who spent their childhood at the Westminster School in London automatically got scholarships. It helped to have friends with influence at the Royal Court. Newton had none.

Newton knew it was time to catch up on his homework. His notes reveal that he went back to review books that he should have read when he first came to university. Again,

✤ Isaac Barrow was the first Cambridge professor to hold the Lucasian Chair of Mathematics. Isaac Newton and other distinguished scholars have followed Barrow through the years.

From Renaissance to a Royal Society

When Johannes Gutenberg invented the printing press in 1440, European learning exploded in a renaissance, shaking itself loose from medieval ways. *Renaissance* means "rebirth," and a new breed of scientists blossomed.

Before the 1800s, scientists called themselves "natural philosophers." Many natural philosophers studied all the fields of science and learned practically everything written about each subject, nearly impossible for a scholar today.

In the mid-1600s, gentlemen formed clubs to share their excitement about natural philosophy. When Isaac Newton was young, London scholars began to discuss the latest discoveries in science. Once King Charles II joined this group, it took the name "The Royal Society." Quickly the Society and its journal, the *Philosophical Transactions*, became England's top authority in scientific matters.

To be elected a Fellow (a member) of the Royal Society was an honor. Weekly demonstrations of experiments at the Royal Society were key to its success. The idea of experimenting with materials was rather new. When people asked "Why this?" or "Why that?" they expected the reply, "Because that's the way it is." Fixed, absolute ideas about nature ruled their thinking.

However, during the Society's early days, natural philosophers adopted the suggestions of Francis Bacon, an English philosopher. Bacon urged scholars to change their worldview of fixed ideas. So they turned the process around. First they made observations and recorded them. Then they spent time thinking about these observations. After that, they offered hypotheses (statements) to explain what they saw. Finally, they used experiments to test their ideas and went on to state their conclusions.

The fellows of the Royal Society never realized that they helped create the Scientific Revolution as they gradually developed the scientific method.

❈ (RIGHT) William Harvey, an English physician and natural philosopher, discovered that blood circulates throughout the human body. (FAR RIGHT) Francis Bacon (1561–1626)

though, Newton totally neglected the basics of Euclid's geometry. When Dr. Barrow gave Newton an oral exam on Euclid's work, Newton couldn't explain simple geometry to the esteemed professor at all. Dr. Barrow had no clue that Newton understood Descartes' much more difficult analytical geometry because Newton never told him.

For whatever reasons, Newton won himself a scholarship. Maybe Dr. Barrow saw promise in Newton as a scholar, despite Newton's terrible performance in geometry. At some point, Newton must have impressed Dr. Barrow with his grasp of mathematics. Perhaps others also recognized that Newton was smarter than the rest. Most likely, he had a mentor with influence at Cambridge in the form of Dr. Humphrey Babington. Babington was rector of a church near Woolsthorpe and a senior fellow—an upper-level teacher—at Trinity. Dr. Babington's sister was married to Mr. Clark, the apothecary in Grantham, and Newton had lived with the Clarks during his days at the King's School. Quite possibly Dr. Babington put in a good word for Newton with the fellows at Trinity College.

Newton was now a graduate of Trinity College and on his way to earning a master's degree. However, not one person in all of Trinity College or Cambridge University, including Drs. Barrow and Babington, still had any hint that Isaac Newton's brain held uncommon genius.

Pests, Plague, and the Wonder Years

In the spring of 1665, as he studied for his exams, Newton heard frightening news. Londoners were dying of the plague. England's most feared disease, the plague struck several times during the 1600s. People had good reason to be alarmed. In the 1300s, the plague had swept through Europe like fire through a house of straw. By the time it faded away, one of every three men, women, and children was dead. The plague became known as the "Black Death."

People in Newton's Cambridge had no idea that the plague was caused by a deadly relationship between two everyday pests—black rats and fleas. In the 1600s, both thrived across Europe. Fleas lived alongside families in every household, rich or poor. Black rats hid in thatched roofs and building walls. Rats ate garbage, and every town had garbage to spare.

Black rats carried plague. Fleas need blood meals from a host animal, and when fleas in search of a meal bit black rats, they became infected with plague as well. A bite from an

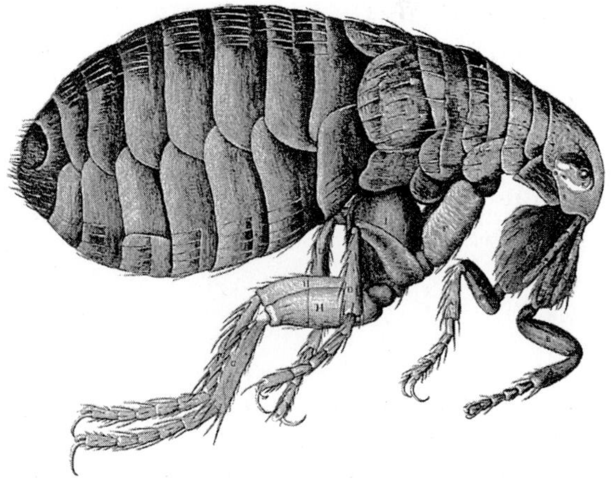

❖ A giant image of a flea drawn by Robert Hooke, a member of the Royal Society.

infected flea transferred plague into an unlucky person's bloodstream.

Not even Isaac Newton could guess that a type of bacteria carried plague from a rat to a flea to a human victim. No one even knew that bacteria existed. More than two hundred years would pass before doctors used microscopes to identify bacteria that caused the plague.

Then the plague arrived in Cambridge, in the company of travelers and the fleas that rode along in their woolen clothes. The summer of 1665 was unusually warm and humid for a city so far north. The hot, sticky weather made a perfect climate for fleas to thrive.

The plague was horrific. People ran high fevers as infected glands in their armpits, groins, and necks swelled to the size of dried purple plums. Victims' brains were affected, and many of the sick went out of their minds, running madly through the streets. Once city authorities discovered them, they nailed their doors shut, imprisoning not only the victims but everybody else inside. A red

✤ An early woodcut depicts the devastation of the plague.

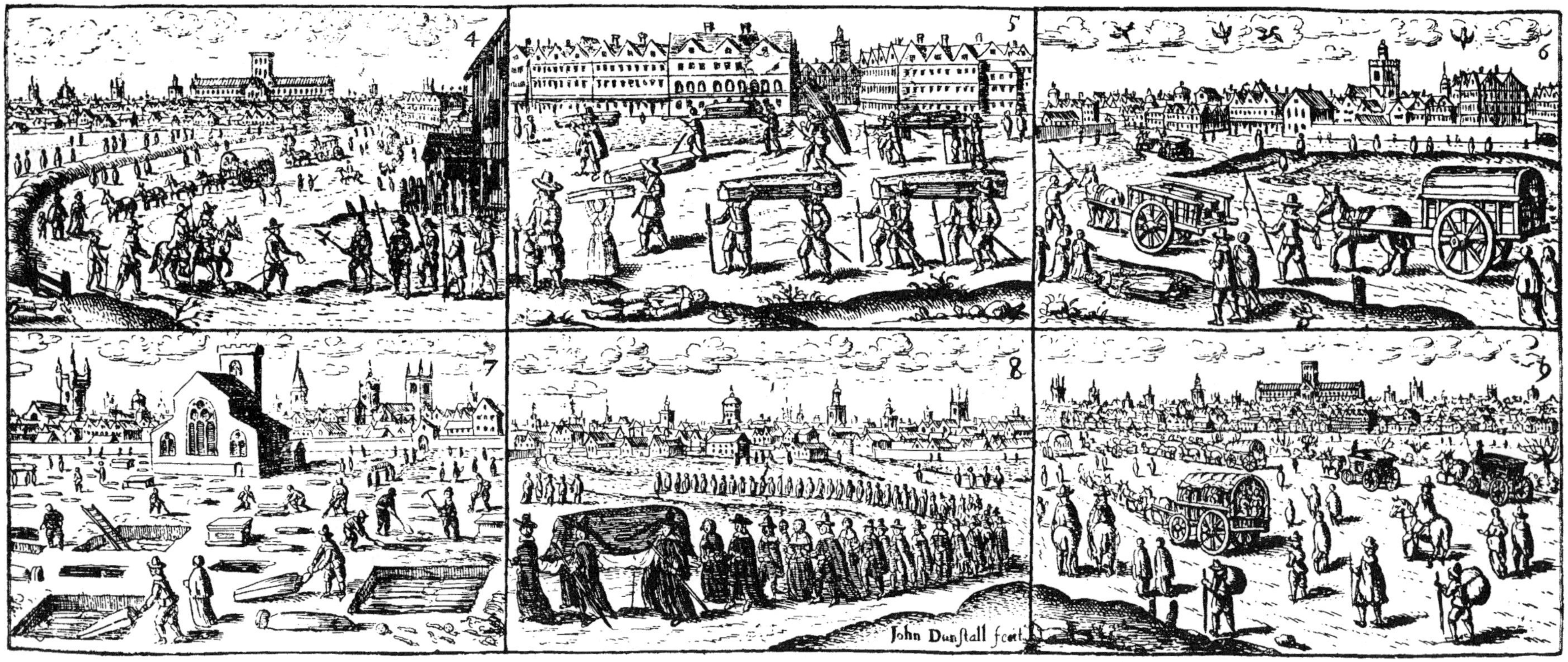

cross slashed across the door told everyone outside that the plague had struck.

If 10 people in a household became sick, only two or three would survive. Nurses were supposed to care for them, but everyone complained that they did nothing but steal from those they were supposed to help. Every night during that hot summer, body collectors called out for the dead as they drove carts through the streets to haul corpses to cemeteries and dump them in mass graves.

Many remedies were offered, and people were willing to try anything to keep from becoming infected. They burned fires to ward off the "bad air" they believed carried the disease. They wore bundles of herbs like rosemary, mint, and wormwood around their necks and grew herbs in their windows. Sometimes they fired guns in their homes, hoping that the stench of gunpowder would kill the vile, evil pestilence. A Cambridge doctor even suggested that healthy citizens wear a tiny piece of excrement from a plague victim in a bag around the neck to ward off the disease.

By summer's end, most Cambridge students and their tutors had escaped the city to smaller villages to continue their study. Isaac Newton, who didn't need a tutor, simply went home to Woolsthorpe.

Quiet Time in Woolsthorpe

The plague died away during cold weather, so Cambridge University opened the following March, and Newton returned. But with the coming of another warm summer, the plague struck again, and once more he left the university. For the better part of two years, from 1665 until 1667, Newton lived in Woolsthorpe. With nothing to prove to teachers and no distractions of life in a noisy college, Newton seemingly thrived.

Among historians who wrote about Newton until the early 1900s, it was fashionable to refer to this period as Newton's *anni mirabili*, his "miracle years." Recent historians, however, took a less romantic, more objective view and found that Newton's miracle years weren't miraculous at all. Four years of learning at Cambridge had filled Newton's mind. Left alone at Woolsthorpe, Isaac Newton could simply do what he did best: think and wonder.

Newton used his two years at Woolsthorpe to let everything bubble up inside his head. All he had learned at Cambridge about natural philosophy and mathematics now fermented like yeast in the bread and beer he had for breakfast. During the day, he could look into the garden and watch apple trees blossom into fruit that ripened and fell to

❖ Plague doctors wore long waxed gowns and beaked masks filled with herbs to ward off disease as they visited their patients. Franklin Mint

MAKE A PLAGUE MASK

DOCTORS IN THE Middle Ages and during Isaac Newton's time wore long waxed overcoats and masks when they made house calls. They stuffed the "beaks" of their masks with herbs in the hope that these might prevent them from catching the plague, as well. Versions of these masks are very popular in cities that celebrate Mardi Gras or Carnival before the Christian season of Lent begins.

You can try your hand at making yourself a plague mask. Add a coat, sweatshirt, and hat, and you'll have a terrific costume.

YOU'LL NEED

- Scissors
- Pencil
- Poster board
- Ruler
- Tape
- Face mask (perhaps two nested together if the mask is flimsy)
- Plain piece of paper
- Colored markers
- Hooded sweatshirt
- Old adult's coat, like a raincoat
- Floppy hat

Enlarge the patterns on the facing page to draw full-sized paper patterns for the top and bottom of your mask. On the grid, one square equals one inch. (Hint: The bottom beak is 11 inches long, exactly as long as a regular piece of computer paper.)

Cut out the paper patterns. Then use them to trace both triangles onto the poster board. Cut these out.

For the top of the beak, use the ruler and one edge of your scissors to "score" a line down the center of the wide triangle. Fold the triangle in half along the scoring line.

Tape one edge of the large triangle to one long side of the small triangle. Place them on your work area tape-side up. Then lay another strip of tape along the other edge of the large triangle, leaving half of the tape exposed.

Fold up your beak and use your fingers to seal it shut. The taped edges should all be on the inside of the beak.

Here comes the tricky part! Most likely you'll have spaces at the lower outside corners of your beak. Mount the beak onto the face mask so that the eyeholes stay clear. There will be some gaps between the mask and the lower corners of the beak. But if you look carefully, you can see how the curve of the face needs to fit the beak. Trim a small curve away from the underside of the beak so that it fits the mask. If they still don't fit right, trim away a little more at a time until you get a good fit.

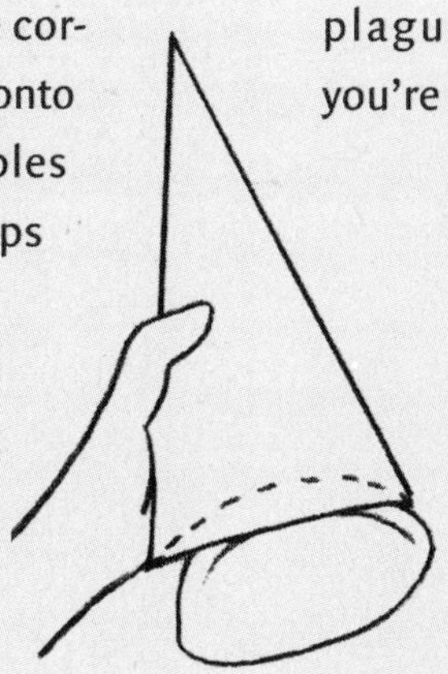

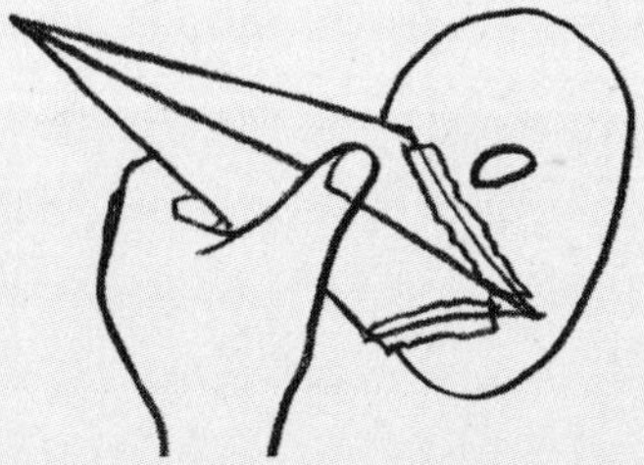

Using short strips, tape the beak to the mask. Work carefully and try to keep the tape smooth. Trim off any extra tape.

Decorate your mask any way you like. Use markers to add details. Old pictures of plague masks often show mouths or nostrils on the beaks, as well as "spectacles" around the eyes. Use your imagination!

To give the full effect, first put on the hooded sweatshirt, then the old coat. Put on your mask, and then a floppy hat. Now you're a plague doctor, and you're good to go!

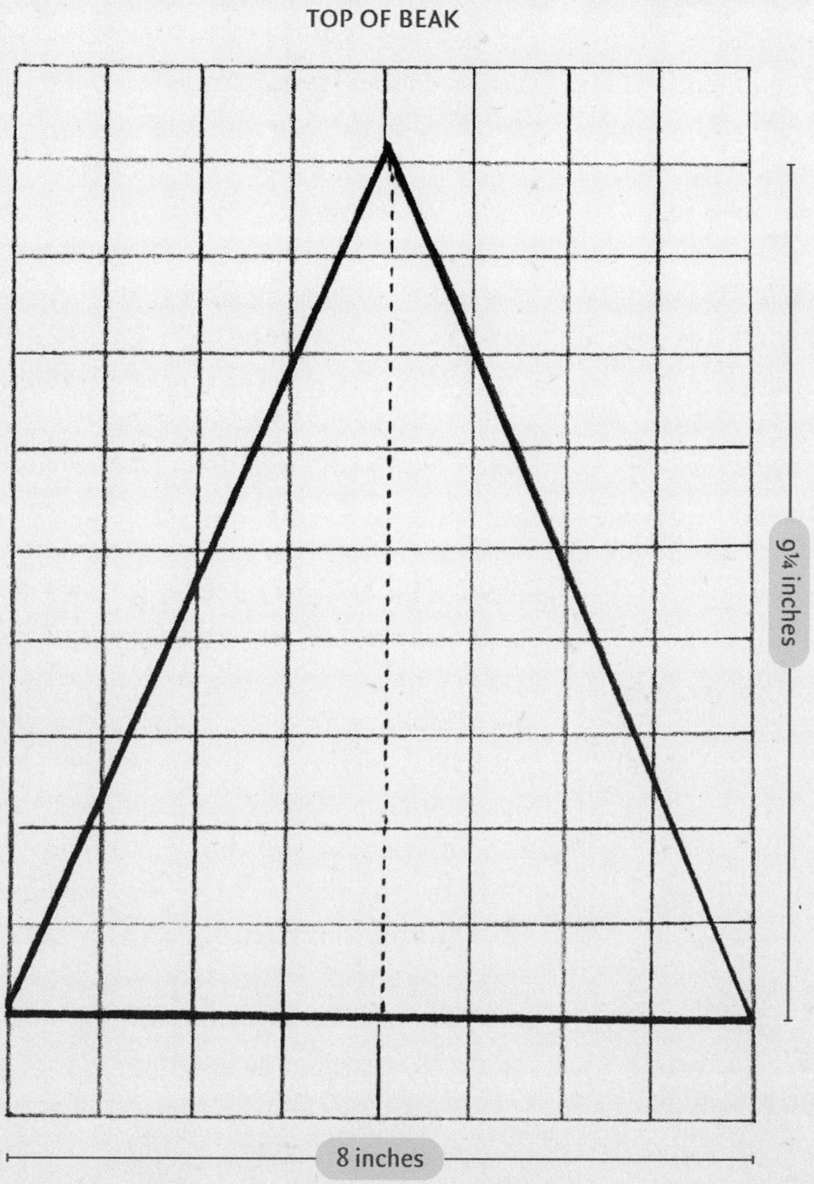

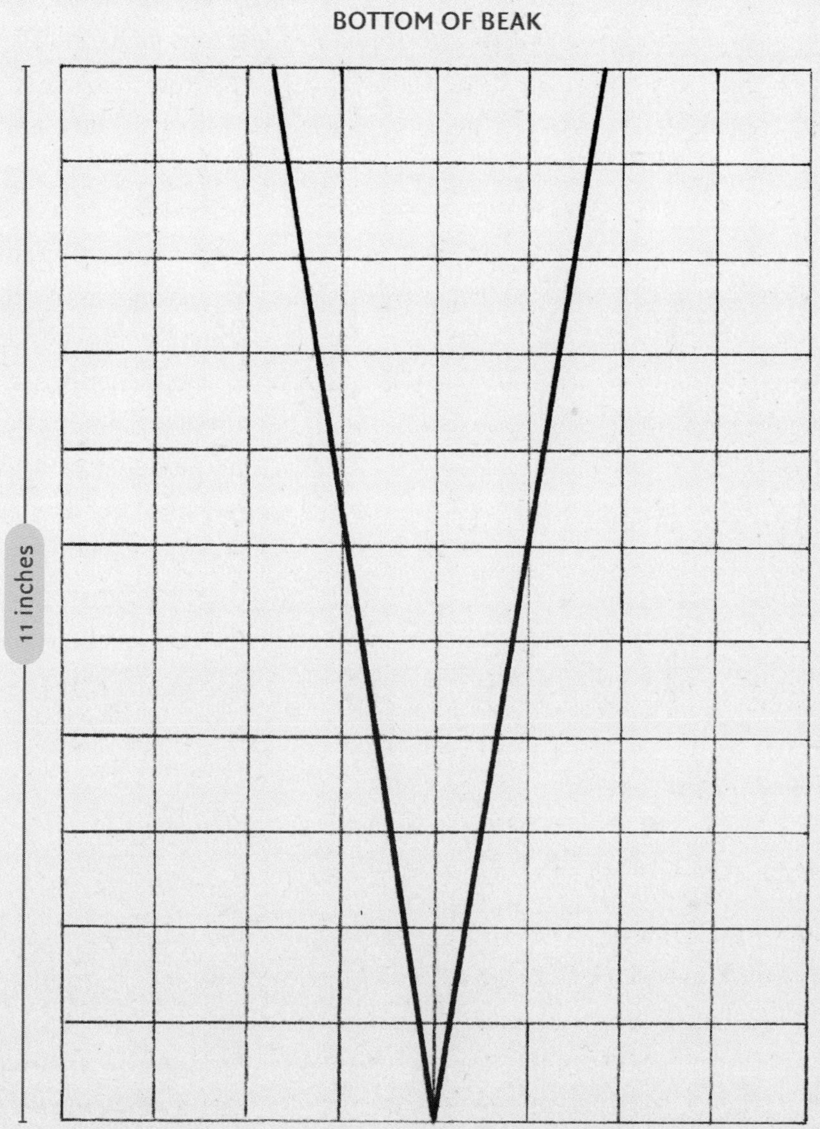

1 square = 1 inch

the ground. When it rained, he could wonder why rainbows appeared. At night, he still watched the heavens for stars and planets, just as he had when he was a boy.

Quiet time gave Newton a chance to reflect on all he had learned. What was more, he had finished growing up. He had started Cambridge at age 18. Now he was 22, a man with a maturing mind. Nothing could stop him from asking more and more about the universe. Just like a great artist or magnificent composer, Newton was driven by a powerful need to create. He did not create paintings, nor did he write symphonies. Newton created questions that started right outside his window and reached to the farthest points in space:

Why do things always fall down?

Why doesn't the moon fall down onto the earth?

How fast does a cannonball fly before it starts to fall to earth?

Why do comets fly by Earth at regular intervals?

Why do planets stay in orbit?

✤ A rainbow appears over Newton's historic home in Woolsthorpe. Roy Bishop

Isaac Newton was beginning to grapple with the concept of motion. Back in Cambridge, Newton had realized that mathematics could help him find the answers to these questions. For a time during his years at home, he pushed this thinking further.

Newton wrote papers that discussed curves and how to do the math in order to find the area under them. These mathematical skills would help him solve problems about moving objects. He called his new form of math *fluxions*, which later became known as "calculus."

Newton did not work miracles during his months of retreat from the plague, but they certainly were his "wonder years." Newton wondered, and he asked questions.

Then he set about to answer them.

CHAPTER 5

THE LIGHT SHINES ON ISAAC NEWTON

IN THE SPRING of 1667, Isaac Newton returned to Cambridge. In London, the Great Fire had burned the city to the ground in 1666. All through England, it seemed that the plague had burned away as well.

Newton continued his odd ways. Beyond sharing quarters with John Wickins, he made no real friends. He had made incredible advances in his thinking during his years of isolation at Woolsthorpe, but he never volunteered a shred of knowledge. He never told anyone about his work in fluxions. No one had a clue just how far his mind had roamed, or that Newton was well on his way to uncovering the laws governing how planets wander back and forth across the sky.

Early in 1669, Professor Barrow showed Newton a book sent from a London mathematician named John Collins, who circulated messages among math scholars in England and Europe. The book, filled with groundbreaking ideas, was written by a German mathematician named Nicholas Mercator. Mercator's topic was logarithms, a means for mathematicians to use exponents in order to simplify difficult mathematical calculations.

Reading Mercator's published work was enough to jolt Newton out of secrecy. Mercator's book made public about half of the same work that Newton had completed on fluxions at Woolsthorpe, a strong hint that the other half was not far behind. Newton pulled out his notebooks and hurried to write his own treatise, which he entitled *De analysi (Of Analyses).*

Newton's pride overcame his silence. He needed to show the world that his thinking stretched far beyond Mercator's. He willingly shared his paper with Barrow. However, true to form, Newton forbade his professor to send *De analysi* on to Collins. Barrow must have pressured Newton to change his mind by guaranteeing that Collins would send the paper right back. Newton gave in, feeling secure because Barrow agreed to Newton's demand: Newton's name was not to appear on the manuscript.

Collins was an ordinary, but passionate, scholar of math. He saw instantly that Newton's paper was dazzling, and his positive comments appeared to ease Newton's anxiety. Finally, Newton agreed to put his name on the paper.

Collins kept his word and returned Newton's paper to Barrow—but first he was prudent enough to copy it by hand. He also wrote letters about Newton's work to other mathematicians in England and abroad. Whether Isaac Newton liked it or not, his name began to spread beyond the walls of Trinity College and Cambridge University.

Professor Newton Lectures on Light

In 1669 Professor Barrow resigned his professorship at Trinity College to take his place as a clergyman in the Church of England—the next step for a Cambridge professor. He nominated Newton, who had completed his master's degree the previous year, to take his place.

When Newton became the new Lucasian Professor of Mathematics, he was able to drop his tiresome job as tutor for a group of bored students. A professor's task was to write and deliver a lecture each week during the term and then to file a copy of it in the Cambridge library. Predictably, Newton's bright ideas went right over the heads of students, as well as many teachers at Cambridge. No one sat taking notes during his lectures. Often, students and other faculty passing by the lecture hall would see Newton there alone, decked out in his scarlet gown, speaking to an empty room. Professor Newton was "lecturing to the walls," as one passerby explained things.

Isaac Newton could have lectured on any one of his many passions, such as mathematics or the laws of motion. Either was a valid topic for a natural philosopher in the late 1600s. No one knows for certain why the young professor decided that his first lectures would cover optics, the study of light. Nonetheless, this topic captivated natural philosophers of all stripes.

As early as 300 B.C., the ancient Greeks understood a basic principle of light. The Greek mathematician Euclid (YEW-klid) knew that a ray of light follows a simple rule:

The Angle of Incidence (Incoming Light) = The Angle of Reflection (Outgoing Light)

For example, when a ray of light falls onto a mirror at a certain angle, the mirror reflects the light away at the same angle—when looked at from the opposite direction. (The same thing happens when you throw a rubber ball against a wall.)

There was another rule in optics that Newton understood. In 1621, well before Newton's birth, a Dutchman named Willebrord Snell discovered the "Sine Law of Refraction." However, Rene Descartes, the French scientist, became the first to put the sine law into print. Snell and Descartes observed that light is bent when passing through certain materials. This phenomenon is called "refraction."

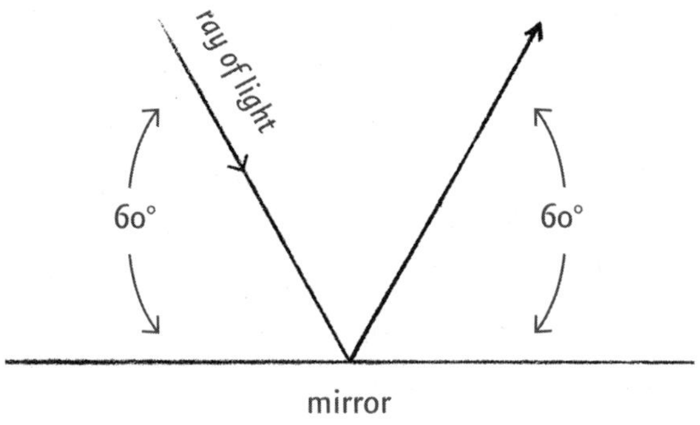

You can observe refraction for yourself by placing a stick in a pool of water. The stick appears to be bent, because the water refracts the light. Descartes said that a refracted ray of light follows these rules:

Light is bent according to the composition and thickness of the material it is going through.

and

There is a constant ratio (relationship) *between the angle of the light as it enters the medium and the angle of light once it is bent.*

Isaac Newton agreed with Descartes' thinking about refraction. However, when it came to the theory of how a beam of white light breaks into colors, Newton parted company with Descartes.

Descartes believed that when light passes through a material, the material itself, which he called a "medium," changes the light into different colors. He wrote that white light is a pure, unchanging form. However, Descartes

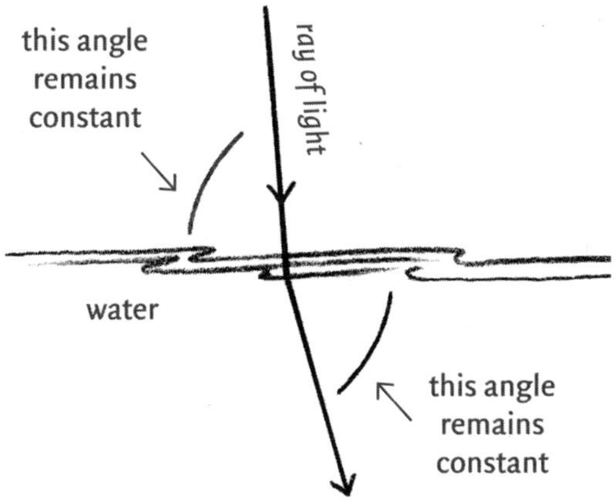

never did any experiments to prove whether his ideas were correct. He based his work on beliefs he already had about light and how it behaves. He never tested his ideas in a scientific manner.

During his years of withdrawal at Woolsthorpe during the plague, Newton had experimented with light. At a big country fair, Newton possibly spotted a set of prisms—solid glass triangles that appear to break up sunshine. He took them home and began to experiment with them. To prove his theory, he placed a prism in a darkened room. Newton arranged the window shutters so that a tiny beam of light shot through it, landing on a wall 20 feet across the room.

Newton then examined the tiny spot on the wall. There sat a rectangular rainbow comprising seven colors, what we call the "spectrum" of red, orange, yellow, green, blue, indigo, and violet. Newton was convinced that white light is made up of distinct colors. He wrote that "Light it self is a heterogeneous mixture of differently refrangible rays." In other words, as a ray of white light flows through a prism, the light is broken up into the spectrum.

To prove that point, Newton took things further. He left the first prism where it was and placed a second prism several feet beyond the first. Then he drilled tiny holes into two boards. He set the boards between the prisms, one board just beyond the first prism and the second board in front of the second prism. Newton then rotated the first prism so that it could refract just one color of the spectrum through the holes in both boards and then through the second prism.

If Descartes' ideas were correct, then the second prism should change that one color of light yet again. But it didn't. Red light refracted through the first prism stayed red after it flowed through the second. The same thing happened with blue light at the other end of the spectrum.

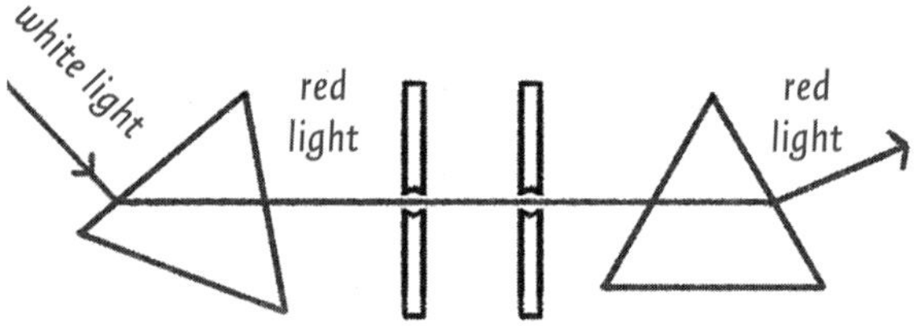

Newton now knew for certain that white light comprises all the colors visible to the naked eye. (In the 1900s, physicists went on to learn that there is an entire electromagnetic spectrum of light waves that we cannot see including microwaves, x-ray waves, infrared waves, and TV waves.)

What was more, Newton watched as each refracted color always was bent at the same angle. A ray of blue was bent at the sharpest

❖ Newton analyzing a ray of light.

MAKE A PRISM

YOUNG ISAAC NEWTON was lucky enough to buy a prism at a country fair so he could experiment with sunlight. Perhaps you have a prism at home. If not, here's a simple and fun way to make one yourself. This experiment works best on a clear, sunny day.

YOU'LL NEED

- Flat pan or dish of water (glass container works best)
- Sturdy white paper or cardboard
- Flat mirror
- Piece of clay (or other object to prop your mirror)

Place a shallow container of water in direct sunlight, near a window. Stand a sheet of white paper or cardboard between the window and the container.

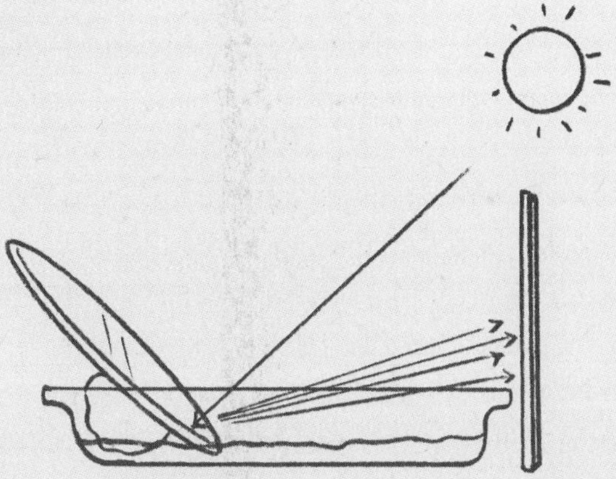

Place the mirror into the water at the back of the dish. Adjust the angle of the mirror until you see a "rainbow" on your paper. Then, use a piece of clay to keep the mirror steady.

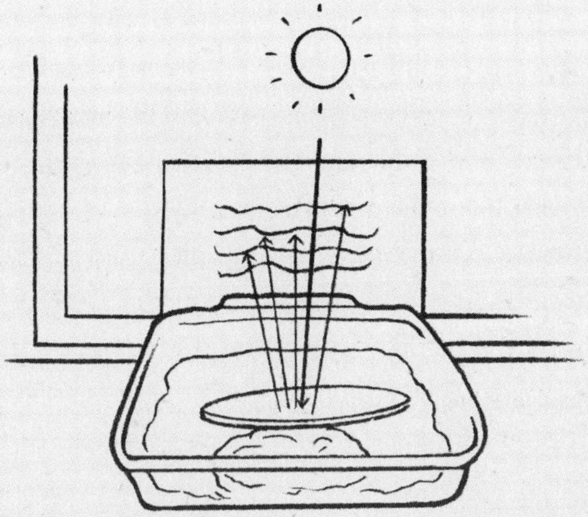

What's happening? The rainbow you see is the spectrum—the seven colors that combine to make white light. Until Newton published his *Opticks*, most scientists thought that prisms somehow transformed white light into different colors.

Newton, however, said that white light is a combination of seven colors, always in the same order: red, orange, yellow, green, blue, indigo, and violet. (Indigo is the color of dark blue denim jeans.) To help you remember, physicists have grouped the first letter of each color into a man's name:

R	O	Y	G.	B	I	V
E	R	E	R	L	N	I
D	A	L	E	U	D	O
	N	L	E	E	I	L
	G	O	N		G	E
	E	W			O	T

The mirror bounces the sunlight as it moves through the water, making the "wedge" of water act the same way the glass of a prism does, refracting white light into the spectrum you see on the paper.

What would happen if you added red, yellow, or blue food coloring to the water? Try it!

angle; a ray of red was bent much more gently. This discovery became enormous once Newton applied mathematics to the refraction of light. He saw that, as white light travels through a prism and is broken up into the spectrum, each color travels not only in its own direction, but also at its own speed.

Years later, Newton called this his *experimentum crucis*—his "crucial experiment." Newton had hypothesized, observed, measured, and recorded his findings on paper, building on Francis Bacon's ideas about the scientific method. All the years of watching rainbows and tinkering with prisms had burst into a new idea: white light wasn't pure at all. Newton was so convinced that he was correct he posed this new idea as not just a hypothesis, but as a theory. He knew his idea was right.

A New View on the Telescope

NEWTON performed other experiments to test his ideas. As he placed lenses on top of other lenses, or placed curved lenses on top of flat glass surfaces, he made notes of how they refracted light. Newton also attacked a problem known as "chromatic aberration," which had annoyed Galileo as he built his telescopes.

Galileo applied the concept of refraction in his telescopes by using one lens to capture light from a distant object and another lens to refract it into an eyepiece. Troublesome fringes of light appeared around these images.

Newton tackled the obstacle of chromatic aberration by completely redesigning the telescope. He used a concept developed—but never built—by Scottish astronomer James Gregory and drew up plans for a reflecting telescope. He chose a tiny concave mirror to capture light and *reflect* it into a second mirror. This mirror then reflected the light through an eyepiece.

All that Newton had learned as a boy building tiny waterwheels and paper lanterns served him well; he was not only a gifted scientist but also an expert artisan. With his own hands, Newton built the telescope of beech wood and brass. Inside it he placed a tiny metal mirror just two inches in diameter.

The mirror was Newton's handiwork as well. He chose metal as a material because it was easier to work with than glass—Newton needed to be sure that his mirror curved to his exact specifications. At home in his chambers, Newton used a furnace to melt copper, tin, and highly toxic arsenic into an alloy that he could mold and then grind into a mirror.

Newton wrote about the process in a letter to the Royal Society, referring to himself in the third person:

The way, which he used, was this. He first melted the Copper alone, then put in the Arsenick, which being melted, he stirred them a little together, bewaring in the mean time, not to draw in breath near the pernicious fumes. After this, he put in Tin, and again so soon as that was melted (which was very suddenly) he stirred them well together, and immediately powred [poured] *them off.*

Newton had circumvented the problem of chromatic aberration. Even more revolutionary was the size of his new telescope—it could fit in his hand, yet it magnified objects nearly 40 times. Better, Newton wrote, "Yesterday I compared it with a six foot Telescope, and found it not only to magnifie more, but also more distinctly."

Once Newton allowed his creation into public view, the little telescope caught the fancy of some important people. Astronomers began to send letters asking Newton about his invention. Before long, the Royal Society got wind of it, and at its request, Professor Barrow hand-carried Newton's invention to London in late 1671.

Newton's reflecting telescope caused a huge stir. King Charles himself inspected the night sky with Newton's tiny creation. Shortly thereafter, Isaac Newton was elected to membership in the Royal Society. With no means of registering a patent on Newton's behalf, the group took care to make sure that the young scholar would receive due credit for his work.

Henry Oldenburg, secretary to the Royal Society, sent Newton a letter warning him that unscrupulous inventors might claim the telescope as their own. Oldenburg sent a description of the instrument to Newton so that he "might adde, & alter" the Society's report to make it perfect. Only then would the Royal Society feel free to share with other scientists, especially Christiaan Huygens of Holland, the leading astronomer of the day.

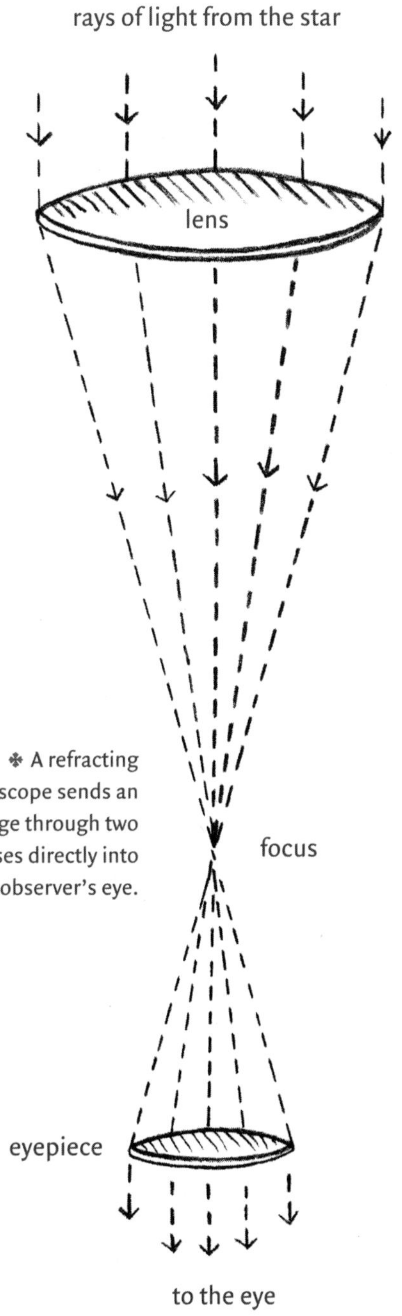

✤ A refracting telescope sends an image through two lenses directly into the observer's eye.

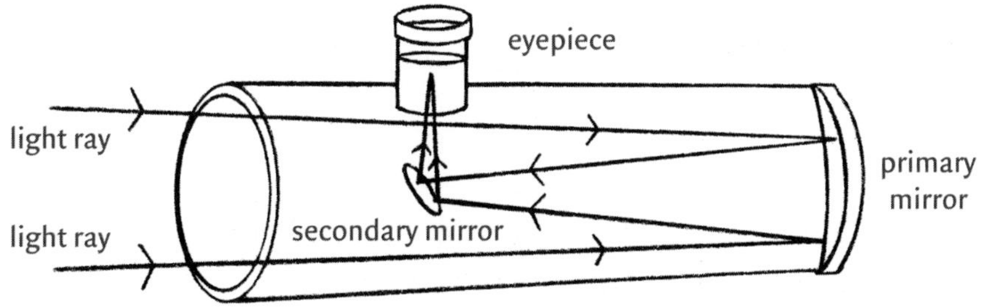

✤ A reflecting telescope captures an image in a concave mirror and reflects it to a second mirror which bounces the image into an eyepiece.

Newton was flattered by the clamor his invention created at the Royal Society. He seemed to feel an unusual sense of security now that the Royal Society had welcomed him into its inner circle, and for a time, his aloofness disappeared. Like a flood breaking through an earthen wall, Newton spilled forth with letters to explain the workings of his little telescope.

Then Newton went further. He promised the Royal Society a letter that would be "an accompt of a Philosphicall discovery wch induced mee to the making of the said Telescope." He promised to share his theories about color with the Royal Society. Indeed, what his little telescope could *do* mattered little to him. More important to Newton was what his telescope represented: Newton's so-

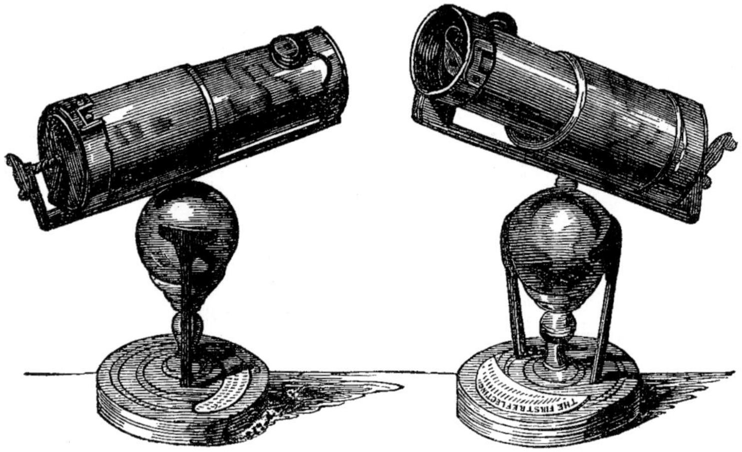

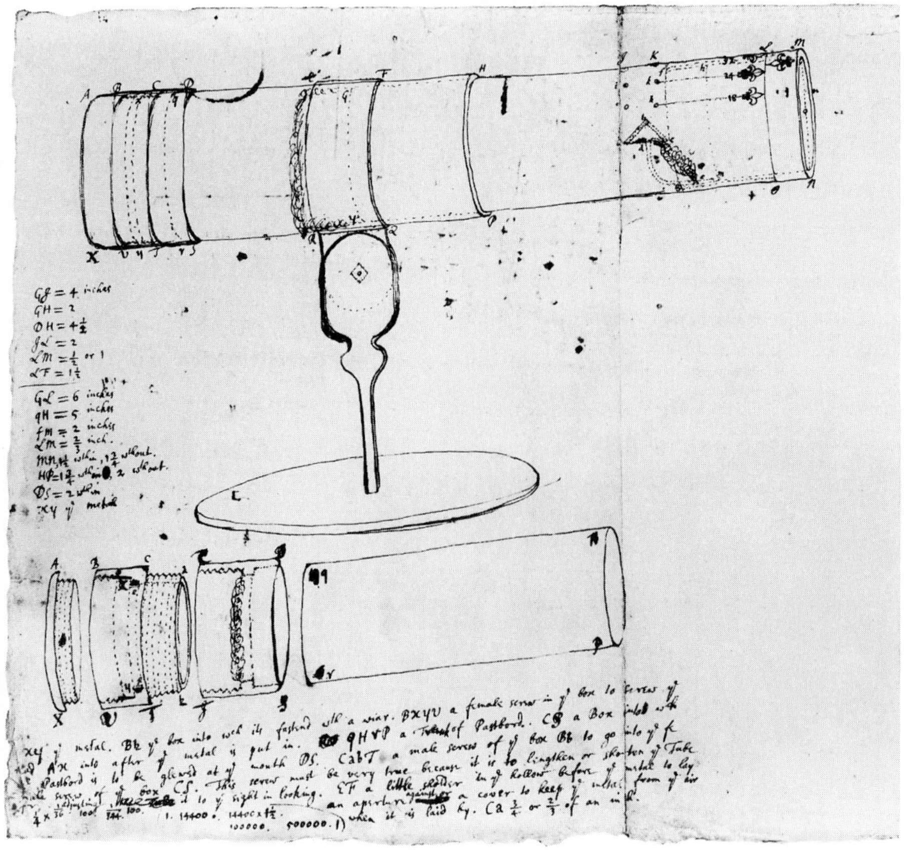

✥ (ABOVE) Newton's reflecting telescope.
(RIGHT) Isaac Newton's sketch of his reflecting telescope.
Library of Congress LC-USZ62-110449

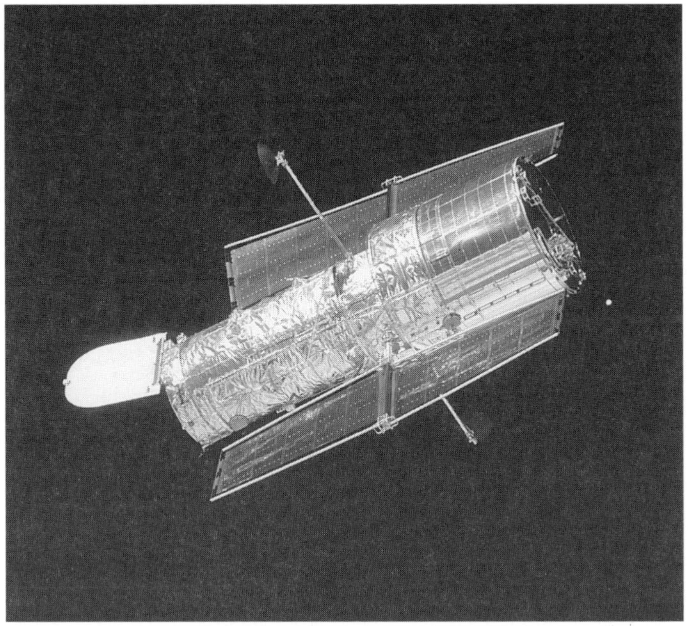

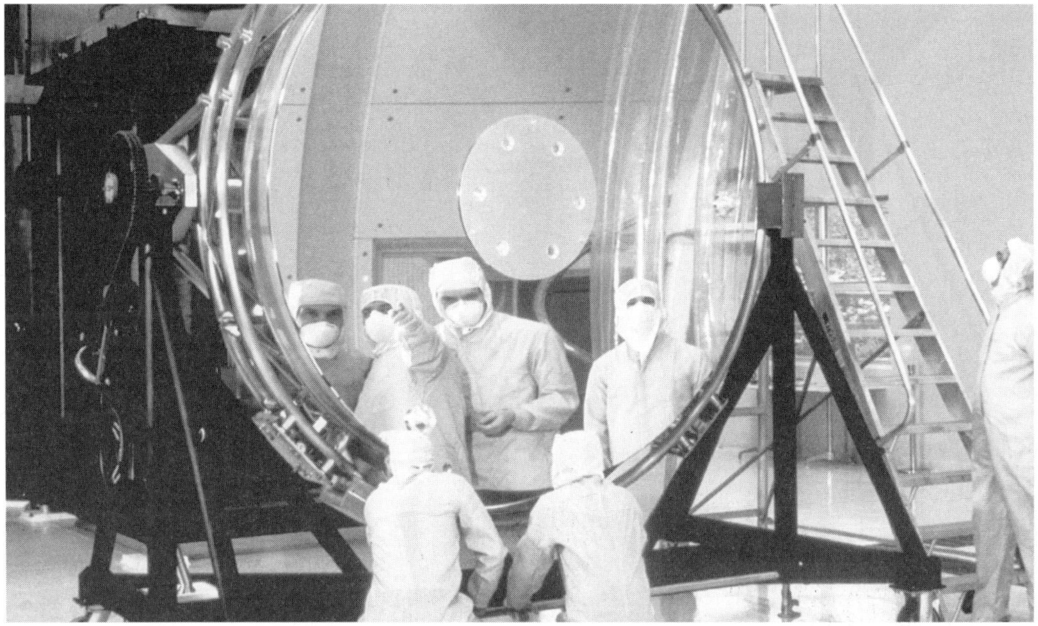

✤ The Hubble Telescope (LEFT) uses an immense concave mirror (detail at right) to capture light from deep space. NASA

lution to the problem of chromatic aberration. Those annoying fringes of light were gone. To Newton, *that* was the discovery. Surely, the natural philosophers of the Royal Society would now eagerly agree with all he had to say about the nature of light.

Newton could not have been more wrong.

A Fight About Light

On February 6, 1672, Isaac Newton sent his first "Letter on Light & Colours" to the Royal Society. The paper was read aloud at the society's next meeting, and Secretary Oldenburg sent Newton a glowing report about the positive comments it received. Flattered, Newton immediately agreed that his paper should go into print. On February 19 Newton's "Letter on Light & Colours" appeared in the Society's *Philosophical Transactions.*

Then the trouble started. What was so obvious to Newton wasn't obvious to others—even to many of the brilliant natural philosophers who met at meetings of the Royal Society.

In those early days of science, there was already a pattern of question-and-answer that continues to this day. Someone offered an idea; others asked questions or offered their own thoughts. Ideas were refined or

even tossed out, progress followed, and new learning grew.

Clearly, the standoffish, awkward Newton could not accept the give-and-take of a hearty debate. England's Astronomer Royal, John Flamsteed, criticized his paper. From Holland came a letter from Huygens praising Newton's work, followed later by Huygens' observations that perhaps Newton wasn't correct, after all. A scholarly Jesuit priest from France, Ignace Gaston Pardies, sent Newton a series of pointed questions that only made clear that the French scientist had no clue to what Newton was talking about.

Newton seemed to be able to shake off criticism from Flamsteed and Pardies, but he reserved a particular distaste for Robert Hooke, an older member of the Royal Society. Seven years Newton's senior, Hooke was well known and the recognized leader in the Royal Society. His book *Micrographia* (*Small Drawings*) had secured Hooke's place in the society as an expert on optics.

Hooke's ideas on the nature of light contradicted Newton's. Hooke wrote a letter to the Royal Society to point out mistakes in Newton's thinking. As Hooke understood from reading Newton's "Letter," Newton believed that light traveled in small pulses that he called "corpuscles," tiny particles that streamed through space. Hooke, on the other hand, was convinced that light travels not in particles, but in waves. Newton's theory on light was wrong, Hooke wrote to the Royal Society, just another unproved claim.

But Hooke had completely missed the point of Newton's letter, and Newton grew ever more frustrated. His paper was about the nature of white light, not that it traveled in particles. In Newton's mind, his theory about light was exactly that, a *theory* which he had *proved* through experimentation. How dare Hooke question that?

Newton blew up. Back and forth angry letters flew, for years. Secretary Oldenburg was caught in the middle of Newton's fury, as he received Newton's letters at the Royal Society and was in charge of making them public. Often he cautioned Newton to temper his nasty comments about Hooke. Sometimes Newton behaved himself, but on other occasions he let fly his contempt for Hooke. What Newton should have seen as professional became personal.

Within months, Newton wrote to Oldenburg that he wished to quit the Royal Society altogether. It took Oldenburg a fair amount of charm to calm Newton down. Oldenburg's flattery worked, and Newton stayed as a member of the Royal Society.

In 1675 Newton journeyed to London where once again he mingled with powerful

Robert Hooke

HISTORIANS HAVE BEEN kinder to Robert Hooke (1635–1703) than Isaac Newton ever was. Hooke, a member of the Royal Society, made remarkable discoveries in natural philosophy: in mathematics, chemistry, architecture, biology, and astronomy.

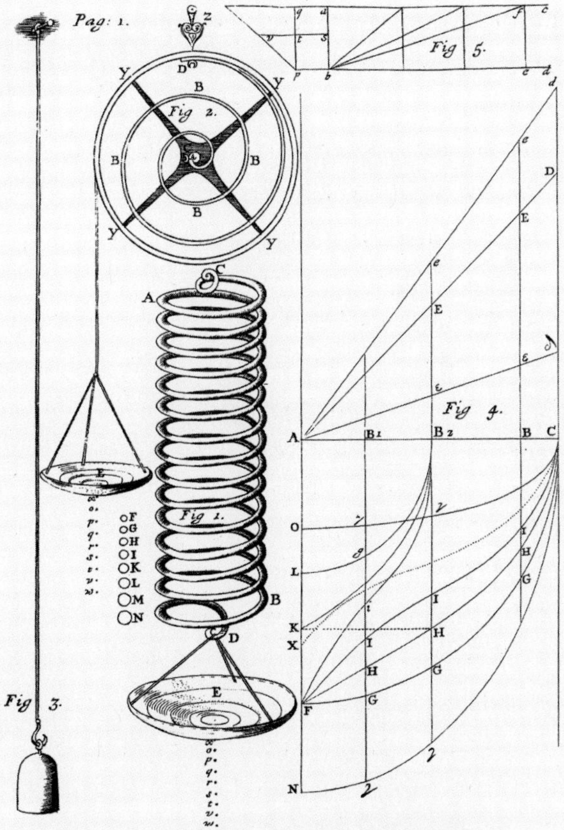

✤ Robert Hooke drew a spring to illustrate his Law of Elasticity. Library of Congress LC-USZ62-110461

In 1660 Hooke announced his Law of Elasticity, which states that the "Power of any Spring is in the same proportion with the Tension thereof." This scientific principle has applications for simple tools people use, like rubber bands, all the way to airframe design on jumbo jets.

Hooke used an early microscope to study nature's secrets and drew his observations. He published them in *Micrographia*, offering wondrous illustrations of everything from snow crystals to common fleas—the first such images in a book. Hooke also deserves credit for using the term *cell*.

✤ Robert Hooke's microscope. Library of Congress LC-USZ62-110443

Hooke was the ideal curator of experiments for the Royal Society. He worked with the architect Christopher Wren to rebuild London after its Great Fire and drew a new street plan for the city. Hooke also designed buildings and probably offered suggestions for Wren's masterwork, St. Paul's Cathedral.

In 1678 Hooke wrote about a scientific rule known as the inverse square law. This principle affects how gravity, light, electricity, and magnetism all behave. Hook was offering his ideas about planetary motion, the same subject that Newton covered in the *Principia* eight years later. However, Newton's astounding skills enabled the mathematics in the *Principia* to easily overshadow Hooke's writings. For the next 25 years, Hooke complained that he deserved some respect from Newton for his scientific work. But Newton refused to give even a shred of credit to Hooke.

When Hooke died in 1703, Newton took over as president of the Royal Society. Rumors spread that Newton had Hooke's portrait destroyed. Yet Robert Hooke's contributions to science live on. People like Hooke, who challenge others' thinking, keep everyone working harder and better.

✤ An ant drawing by Hooke. Library of Congress LC-USZ62-110451

NEWTON'S RINGS

ROBERT HOOKE HOLDS the credit for discovering an optical phenomenon that's named for his archrival, Isaac Newton. As Hooke looked through a microscope to view thin sheets of mica, he saw concentric groups of rings. Mica, a mineral, is made up of thin layers of material separated by layers of air. It transmits light well and at one time served as "glass" in lampshades. Hooke reported on these rings in his book *Micrographia*.

Newton learned about these rings from Hooke and studied them for himself by pressing a lens against a flat piece of glass. He also observed them in soap bubbles and oil slicks. The rings often appear as dark and light circles when light shines through a thin film of air caught between a curved surface and a flat one. Light waves reflect off both edges of the air and interfere with each other. Sometimes Newton's rings are colorful, like a rainbow.

Hooke may have discovered the rings, but only Isaac Newton had the math skills to explain them. As with so many of Hooke's projects, he gets credit for the idea, but the honor goes to another, more famous natural philosopher.

You can observe Newton's Rings (or Hooke's Rings, if you like).

YOU'LL NEED

- Sunny work area (or use a flashlight).
- Concave lens
- Flat piece of clear glass
- Waste Book

Place a lens, concave-side up, over a sheet of glass. "Catch" the beam of sunlight (or shine the flashlight across the lens so that most of the beam of light shines just outside the lens). When you look at the edge of the lens, you should see a series of lines stacked one above the other.

You are observing Newton's Rings—actually a piece of them. Draw a picture of these rings in the lens in your Waste Book.

Depending on where you do your experiment, you might see all kinds of funky reflections that hover above the lens. These aren't Newton's Rings, but they are interesting to observe.

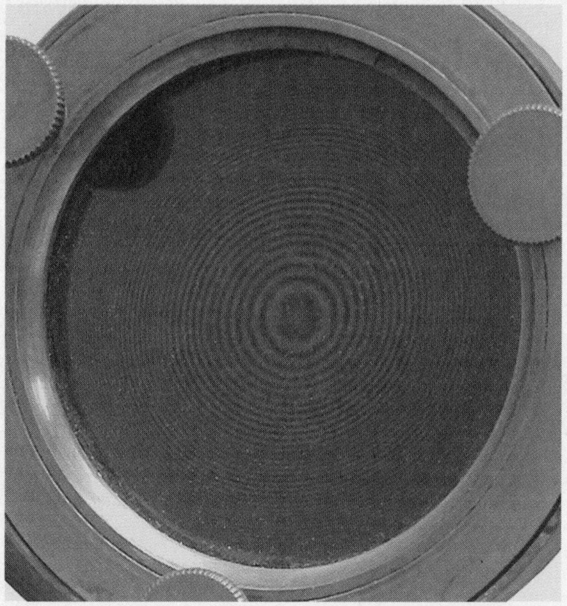

This antique instrument showed college students a view of Newton's rings. You can see the rings for yourself in the enlarged image. Robert Timlin, Allegheny College

men. Perhaps to impress them, Newton went back to Cambridge and prepared two more letters for the Royal Society. One of the letters, "Discourse on Observations," went on to reappear 30 years later in his classic book *Opticks*. The second paper was titled "An Hypothesis explaining the Properties of Light." Newton explained that this paper was his effort to "render ye papers I send you, and other sent formerly, more intelligible [easier to understand]. You may see by the scratching & interlining 'twas done ins hast [haste]," Newton added.

Newton may have written this paper in a hurry, but it dealt with much more than the nature of light. In fact, it was the first time that he exposed his thinking about the nature of the universe to public view. True, "Properties of Light" discussed his ideas on light, but Newton expanded his topics to discussions of chemistry, as well as a mysterious flow of a substance he called "ether" that kept planets in orbit around the sun.

Again Robert Hooke complained, this time charging that many of Newton's ideas had appeared in *Micrographia*. Secretary Oldenburg, whom historians think probably favored Newton over Hooke in their feud, suggested that the two write each other personally. Privately, each one fostered his dislike for the other. Yet, Newton and Hooke appeared to settle their differences and wrote elaborate letters to one another. Their flowery words praised each others' brilliance and the benefits of sharing their thoughts. Newton even went so far as to admit that he owed Hooke's work a huge debt: "If I have seen further it is by standing on ye sholders of Giants."

Perhaps Newton was praising Hooke. But perhaps not. Maybe Newton believed that his work built on the earlier effort of other scientists, the "giants."

Quite possibly Newton was making fun of Hooke. Isaac Newton knew that Robert Hooke was uncommonly short.

A Matter of Mathematics

As Newton was consumed by defending his work on optics, he got word about another mathematician, Gottfried Wilhelm Leibniz (LIBE-nitz), a German whose brilliance shone nearly as bright as Newton's own. At the young age of 20, Leibniz published an essay that laid down the foundation of logic on which today's computers run. Like Newton, Leibniz was a gifted man who studied natural science, philosophy, languages, and theology. Just like Newton—though nearly a decade later—Leibniz developed calculus all on his own. Like Newton, Leibniz was invited to the

✤ Gottfried Wilhelm Leibniz (1646–1716)

✤ Astronomers use calculus to pinpoint the location of any planet in our Solar System. NASA

SHINE YOUR LIGHT ON THE INVERSE SQUARE LAW

AS YOU READ this book, you will come across the term *inverse square law* several times. Isaac Newton used the inverse square law to describe the force of gravity between two objects. As two objects move away from each other, their gravitational pull on each other lessens. When one object doubles its distance from another object, the attraction of gravity between them becomes one-fourth as strong.

Newton also knew that the inverse square law affects how far a light will shine. A star that's twice as far away isn't half as bright, it's one-fourth as bright.

See for yourself the difference distance makes in this activity.

YOU'LL NEED

- Masking tape
- Lamp with a bare bulb
- Tape measure
- Darkened room
- Book

1. Use masking tape to mark several distances from the lamp: place tape marks on the floor 2 feet, 4 feet, 8 feet, and 16 feet (if you have that much room) from the lamp. Use the tape measure to help you.

2. Darken the room and open your book. Stand so that your toes are along the 2-foot mark from the lamp. Can you read your book easily? Step backward and line up your toes at the 4-foot mark. (You are doubling the distance between the 2-foot mark and the 4-foot mark.) What happens? Is the light dimmer? Can you read your book as well?

3. Now step backward to the 8-foot mark. (Again, you are doubling the distance between you and the lamp, but reducing the light level by an inverse square.) What's happened to the light now? Is it brighter or dimmer? Can you read your book?

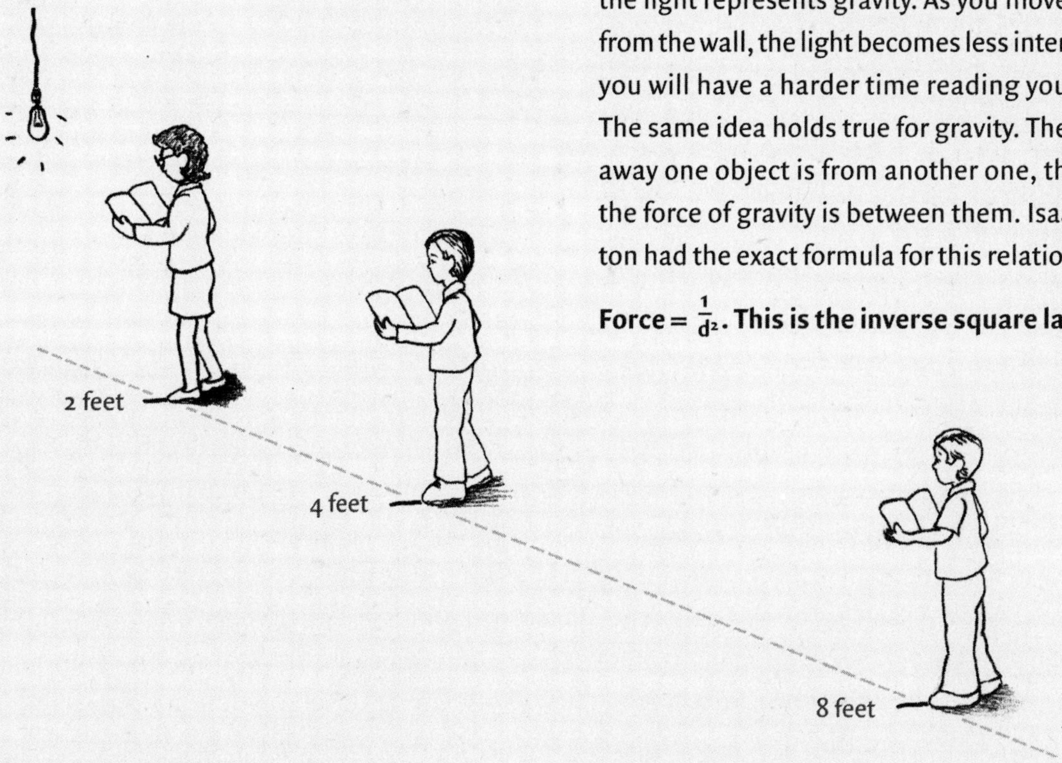

4. If you can, step back until you are 16 feet away from the lamp. (Once again, you are doubling the distance between you and the light source.) Can you read anything at all?

PUT ON YOUR "THINKING CAP." Imagine that the light represents gravity. As you move farther from the wall, the light becomes less intense, and you will have a harder time reading your book. The same idea holds true for gravity. The farther away one object is from another one, the lower the force of gravity is between them. Isaac Newton had the exact formula for this relationship:

Force = $\frac{1}{d^2}$. This is the inverse square law.

Royal Society to show off a novel invention, an automatic calculating machine.

Leibniz wanted to write directly to his mathematical twin. Again Newton refused to deal with Leibniz directly. Instead, he would send letters only through John Collins in London. Once Collins died, contact between the pair was cut off. Preferring to shut himself away in Cambridge, Isaac Newton never learned that Leibniz developed fluxions by himself, just as Newton had. Leibniz called his new branch of mathematics "calculus," the term still used today.

Scholars know that when Leibniz visited London in 1676, Collins gave him a look at Newton's writings on mathematics. Leibniz took notes about things he didn't understand. Importantly, Leibniz did *not* take notes on Newton's writings about fluxions, the reason that historians assume that Leibniz understood them—he had already worked out calculus on his own. This "priority dispute," the argument about who invented calculus first, plagued both men for years.

Newton's refusal to share his knowledge came back to haunt him decades later, when the priority dispute about calculus raged all over Europe. Had Newton actually written Leibniz directly, the pair might well have found a solution to prevent future disagreements.

Calculus

People in many jobs use math in order to observe physical things as they undergo change. For instance, traffic managers study how far a truck will skid, while NASA engineers predict exactly when a robot will touch down on Mars. In each case, researchers apply mathematical calculations to test their hypotheses and work out their conclusions.

Gottfried Leibniz used the term *calculus* to describe this branch of mathematics. *Calculus* and *calculate* rise from the same Latin root word *calx*, a small stone used to keep score in games.

However, Isaac Newton's term *fluxions* also closely described the math we use to study physical changes. *Flux* often refers to the motion of rivers and streams, coming from the Latin *fluere*, "to flow," and *fluus*, "flowing." Have you ever heard an adult say that something is "in flux?" That means that it's in motion and not in its final state.

In truth, Leibniz's calculus and Newton's fluxions were one and the same. They shared interests, too. Leibniz and Newton asked about extremes. How large or long could something expand? How small or short could it shrink? They thought about the concept that a number could be infinitely large or small. They also studied curves, both how curves slope and how to calculate the areas beneath them.

As the 1700s unfolded, more natural philosophers began using calculus in their experiments. Today, students study calculus in high school and college to use for research in everything from physics to business to history itself.

Some researchers think that scholars in India, the "Kerala School," developed basic calculus 250 years before Newton and Leibniz lived. While stacks of manuscripts in Newton's handwriting show that he copied others' works in order to study them, there is no evidence that Newton copied anyone else's work on calculus.

But other matters, mysterious doings that kept him awake for nights on end, were eating away at Isaac Newton, both body and soul.

CHAPTER

THE SECRET YEARS

By 1673, Newton had earned enough influence at Cambridge University to merit extra workspace. A set of wooden stairs led down from his rooms in Trinity College to a garden just outside. Sometimes Newton worked there, scratching math problems or drawings in the gravel walk. He directed the efforts of a gardener who cared for the plants there as well.

But more was going on in that garden. There, secluded by a tall brick wall, Newton kept a private laboratory. Newton himself built a pair of brick and mortar furnaces for heating the ingredients he used in his experiments.

With the exception of John Wickins and whoever kept the place clean, no one ventured inside Newton's secret laboratory. There, Newton surrounded himself with glass phials, crucibles (containers to melt metals), funnels, and flasks. Even the garbage his experiments generated was kept a secret and dumped in a far corner of the garden close to the wall of the Trinity Chapel.

Newton was known to keep secrets, but he had a particular reason to hide this work in his laboratory. Isaac Newton practiced the forbidden art of alchemy.

Alchemy had been practiced since the days of the ancients. Babylonians, Egyptians, East Indians, Chinese, and Arabs all worked in laboratories in pursuit of the same goal, to turn base metals like lead or iron into precious ones like silver or gold. In Europe, alchemists did the same thing, seeking to become masters of great wealth and influence.

Such explorations were kept quiet. At least some alchemists were said to be dabbling in black magic and witchcraft, which gave a bad name to them all. The Church viewed

❖ Isaac Newton's garden in a Trinity College courtyard. Stairs led to his rooms on the second floor.

❖ A medieval woodcut shows an alchemist's furnace.

alchemy as a sin and wrathfully prosecuted those who practiced it. Kings and queens didn't like the idea either—unless an alchemist was looking for ways to provide their majesties with a way to manufacture precious gold and silver. So alchemy was shrouded in mystery, a fact well-suited to Newton's secretive nature.

Alchemists hid other, more mysterious goals. They labored to discover a magical product, a liquid called the "philosopher's stone." They envisioned the philosopher's stone as the "first matter," truly the spark of cosmic being. Such an elixir (liquid) of life, they believed, could heal people who were sick. To discover the philosopher's stone would unlock the secret gate to eternal life. Possess the philosopher's stone, and an alchemist would hold the key to the very mind of God.

Isaac Newton's alchemy took its own unique form. He sought ancient secrets using methods that he created for his own use. Thus Newton applied his own version of the scientific method to alchemy. Unlike other alchemists, Newton actually designed experiments with metals, acids, and bases.

John Wickins fed the charcoal furnaces as Newton carried on his experiments. The furnaces' intense heat enabled Newton to melt lead and other metals in earthenware crucibles. Wickins then helped Newton lift these heavy containers of hot, liquid metal. Curiously, Wickins never seemed to have realized exactly what his chamber-fellow was doing.

Newton went on to combine these molten metals and observed how they became alloys, or mixtures of metals. Sometimes his experiments yielded alloys of gold and silver. With Wickins to assist, Newton set about to discover the properties of metals and what happened when he mixed them with other chemicals such as oil of vitriol (sulfuric acid) or *aqua fortis* (nitric acid).

Newton attacked his work with the intensity of a madman. He toiled long into the night, slept in his clothes, and awoke to start right to work again. He left his chamber to take walks, then turned tail to run back upstairs to write something down in a notebook. He forgot to eat, or would eat his supper, now cold and sticky, for breakfast the next morning.

Newton obviously was far more intent on stirring up his own chemical creations than eating his meals. He sniffed vapors as metals "cooked"—and he tasted his alchemical mixtures once they cooled down. Many of the metals he used, especially mercury and antimony, were highly toxic. Newton was extremely lucky that he did not poison himself or damage his brain.

Newton adopted the symbols of earlier alchemists who named metals after the gods and goddesses of Greek and Roman myths. These pet names mirrored the traits of both the metals and their namesakes. For example, Newton used the ☿ symbol for the metal mercury. Also known as "quicksilver" because it rolls around in a liquid blob at room temperature, mercury took its name from the god Mercury, whose winged sandals carried him with great speed. The mighty god Saturn embodied the dense, heavy properties of lead, while lovely Venus offered her name to the softness and beauty of copper. Newton used other code words as well. In the alchemist's kingdom, gold and silver reigned. Gold was the "sun" and silver the "moon." Gold was "king" and silver "queen."

Newton pored through every alchemy manuscript he could find and copied them to use in his laboratory. Alchemists believed that ancient myths acted as a kind of roadmap, magical trails leading to the formulas one needed to make gold or silver. These manuscripts appeared as long, elaborate poems or fairy tales with symbols of various metals and chemicals taking roles as characters in them.

Alchemists thought that like the great male and female characters in myths, metals had masculine or feminine qualities that must join together to make new creations. One needed only to decode ancient texts to uncover secret recipes for making precious metals out of common ones. Newton had read plenty of myths as he studied the classics at school. He kept them in mind as he scrutinized alchemical manuscripts for clues to their meaning. Then Newton transformed these writings into actual experiments that

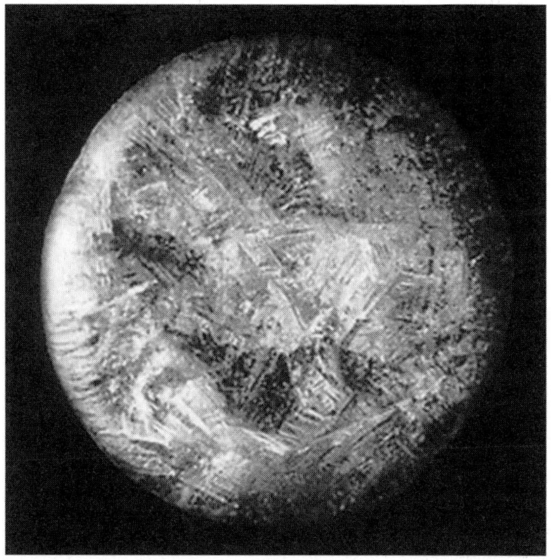

✤ Isaac Newton observed with wonder how the metal antimony, when extracted from ore and treated with iron, transformed into the *star Regulus*, a star-like mineral named for a king. The Chymistry of Isaac Newton, Indiana University

ALCHEMICAL SYMBOLS USED BY ISAAC NEWTON

Alchemical Term	Symbol	Alchemical Term	Symbol	Alchemical Term	Symbol
antimony	♁	last quarter moon	☾	salt of copper	🜠
antimony ore	♁°	lead ore	♄	antimoniate	
aqua fortis	🜅	Mars (iron)	♂	Scorpius	♏
Aquarius	♒	oil	🝆	sulfur	🜍
Aries	♈	ounce sign	℥	gold (sun)	☉
bismuth	♆	Pisces	♓	tin (Jupiter)	♃
(Neptune, Trident)		recipe	℞	tin ore	♃
Cancer	♋	salt	⊖	vinegar	🜊
Inverted Leo	♌	salt of antimony	♁	white hourglass	⧖
iron ore	♂°				

he conducted hidden behind his garden wall at Trinity College.

Of course, Newton was never a garden-variety alchemist. His strong skills in mathematics, as well as his zest for actually experimenting with metals and chemicals, gave him an advantage. Isaac Newton grew to understand that, even in alchemy, real chemical processes were taking place.

As with every other topic that interested him, Newton began a notebook to record his work in alchemy. Over the 30 years that Newton lived and worked at Trinity College in Cambridge, he performed some 400 alchemical experiments. Newton's study also resulted in the *Index Chemicus* (*Chemical Index*), a guidebook to all the writings he discovered about alchemy. With 879 headings, 5,000 page references, and references to 100 other authors, it was clear that Newton knew his subject inside and out.

Alchemy conjures up images of wizards and snakes and boiling cauldrons of strange potions. But this was not what Isaac Newton was up to, nor does it seem that Newton practiced alchemy just because he wanted to turn lead into gold. Most likely, Newton searched for secrets of a more spiritual nature. He was on the hunt for the philosopher's stone itself.

By practicing alchemy, Newton yearned to find the "first matter," universal truths that tied up everything in the cosmos into one neat package that was simple to explain. Isaac Newton was convinced that simplicity reigns.

✤ Alchemists chose the Greek god Jupiter to represent the properties of tin, a metal. When you shake a thin sheet of tin, it rumbles like the sound of thunder, one of Jupiter's features. Library of Congress LC-USZ62-123889

Chymistry

Although Isaac Newton was willing to go public with his work on the theory of light in 1675, he made certain that no light was ever shed on his alchemy. Two centuries passed

Translate an Alchemist's Poem

ONE OF THE scores of manuscripts that Isaac Newton read about alchemy included a poem by Basil Valentine. This long-dead alchemist was supposedly a monk who published under his colorful nickname. Valentine wrote many papers about alchemy, and Newton hand-wrote copies of them for his own collection, including the poem from *Mystery of the Microcosm*.

Newton probably read the poem in German or Latin and translated it into English—early modern English! Try your hand at translating it into 21st century English. What is Basil Valentine saying? (Turn your book upside down to see a suggested translation.) The poem hints at the secret goal that Newton and so many other alchemists sought.

Here are some hints to help you: You might find it interesting to use a dictionary that gives the etymology (history) of words. Key words in Valentine's poem are underlined. Unfamiliar words are followed by their definitions in brackets. Gold, silver, mercury, copper, iron, tin, lead, and antimony were metals that Isaac Newton tested in his laboratory. "Green" was used for all kinds of meanings dealing with life and growth, as well as for copper, which appears green when found in the ground.

The Philosopher [alchemist] speaketh thus.
Bright glorious king of all this world, o Sun,
Whose progeny's [children's] upholder is the Moon,
Both whom Priest Mercury does firmly bind [marry],
Unles Dame Venus favour you do find,
Who for her spous [spouse] Heroic Mars hath ta'ne [taken].
Without her aid what ere you do's in vain [is of no use].

Jove's [Jupiter's] grace neglect not. Saturn old & grey,
In various hews [hues, colors] will them himself display
From black to white from white again to red
Mounting on stilts he'el walk till he be dead.
And streight [straight] returning into life again
Henceforth in quiet rest he shall remain

Lady in greens cry oh my son most dear
Come Antimony & assist me here.
Come noble salt; come guard me & defend
That worms of me make not a wofull [woeful, sad] end.

SUGGESTED TRANSLATION:

The alchemist has this to say:
Gold and silver are bound together with mercury
With a good result.
In the same way, copper seeks to join with iron.
Without copper, your experiments will have poor results.
Do not forget about experimenting with tin.
Lead will appear in all sorts of colors
From black to white to red. Lead will take all kinds of forms, as well.
Life cries out against death.
Antimony must help her.
Oh come, Philosopher's Stone,
So that I may live forever.

before scholars examined thick sheaves of Newton's papers—one million words' worth of papers—and found out that he was up to some very hush-hush work. Isaac Newton was an alchemist. And he had done a superb job of hiding that fact.

By the time Newton undertook the study of alchemy in the later 1600s, it was crossing over into a brand-new area of science: chemistry, or "chymistry," as Robert Boyle called it. Boyle, another natural philosopher known as the father of modern chemistry, practiced chemistry and alchemy interchangeably. Many of the laboratory techniques he and Newton discovered overlapped both fields.

Boyle was about one generation older than Newton, quite an old man by the time Newton met him at the Royal Society in 1675. Newton knew that Boyle was an alchemist as well as a student of chemistry and began to correspond with him. Their letters reflected their passion for learning—not just the "what" but the "why" of alchemical processes.

Many would not consider alchemy to be a pure science, but there is no doubt that, as alchemists, Boyle and Newton made valuable discoveries. The secrets they studied actually laid a foundation for chemists like Joseph Priestly and Robert Faraday who followed them in the 1700s.

✤ This image is but one person's idea of how God could appear. Library of Congress LC-USZ62-50185

Looking for God

In the early 1670s, Isaac Newton opened yet another notebook and started to write. This time, however, his interests moved beyond natural philosophy to theology: the study of God. Isaac Newton was an intensely religious man. He firmly believed that God was the creator of all things. God's hand, Newton believed, was behind everything the eye could see, from the way planets traveled through the sky to the tiniest chemical changes he observed in his laboratory.

Newton faced inner struggles, too. He had a strong moral compass and worried about the state of his own soul. When he first came to Trinity College at the age of 18 or 19, he made a detailed list of his sins in his notebook during the Easter season. Some of these sins show that Newton had the usual spats with his half-brothers and sisters, as well as with boys at school. Others hint that Newton, even though he was now at the university, had been bitter with anger at his mother for leaving him at Woolsthorpe when she left to marry Barnabas Smith.

As for his 13th sin: Newton was 10 years old when his stepfather died and his mother came back to Woolsthorpe. Obviously, he carried with him sour memories, as well as his sins, for a very long time. Still, Isaac

ISAAC NEWTON'S LIST OF SINS

1. Vsing [Using] the word (God) openly
2. Eating an apple at Thy house [in church]
3. Making a feather while on Thy day [Sunday]
4. Denying that I made it
5. Making a mousetrap on Thy day
6. Contriving of the chimes on Thy day [ringing bells]
7. Squirting water on Thy day
8. Making pies on Sunday night
9. Swimming in a kimnel [tub] on Thy day
10. Putting a pin in Iohn Keys hat on Thy day to pick him
11. Carelessly hearing and committing many sermons
12. Refusing to go to the close at my mothers command
13. Threatning my father and mother Smith to burne them and the house over them
14. Wishing death and hoping it to some
15. Striking many
16. Having uncleane thoughts words and actions and dreamese
17. Stealing cherry cobs [a treat] from Eduard Storer
18. Denying that I did so
19. Denying a crossbow to my mother and grandmother though I knew of it
20. Setting my heart on money learning pleasure more than Thee
21. A relapse
22. A relapse
23. A breaking again of my covenant renued [renewed] in the Lords Supper
24. Punching my sister
25. Robbing my mothers box of plums and sugar
26. Calling Derothy Rose a jade [a nagging woman]
27. Glutiny [Glutony, overeating] in my sickness
28. Peevishness [Irritable] with my mother
29. With my sister
30. Falling out with the servants
31. Divers commissions of alle my duties [Not doing his chores]
32. Idle discourse [talk] on Thy day and at other times
33. Not turning nearer to Thee for my affections
34. Not living according to my belief
35. Not loving Thee for Thy self
36. Not loving Thee for Thy goodness to us

[Newton did not list number 37]

38. Not desiring Thy ordinances [laws]
39. Not long [longing] for Thee…
40. Fearing man above Thee
41. Vsing unlawful means to bring us out of distresses
42. Caring for worldly things more than God
43. Not craving a blessing from God on our honest endeavors
44. Missing chapel
45. Beating Arthur Storer
46. Peevishness at Master Clarks for a piece of bread and butter
47. Striving to cheat with a brass halfe crowne [a coin]
48. Twisting a cord on Sunday morning
49. Reading the history of the Christian champions on Sunday

A Crystal Garden

A READING OF Isaac Newton's work in alchemy shows that Newton believed in "vegetation"—that metals actually grow. In fact, it is often said that minerals like gold, silver, iron, and copper are present in veins of ore that extend in fingerlike deposits below the ground. It seemed reasonable to Newton that minerals grew underground in the same way that plants and trees grow above.

You can use everyday materials to make minerals "grow" right in a dish in your kitchen. As you observe the changes from day to day, you can understand why Newton assumed that minerals vegetate.

Adult supervision required

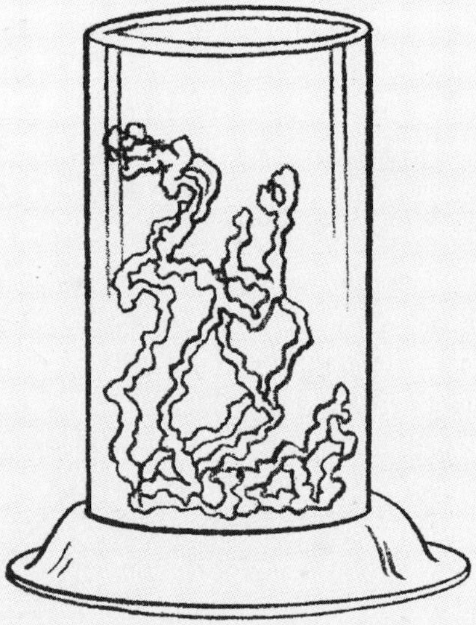

YOU'LL NEED

- Mixing bowl
- 2 tablespoons table salt (*not* iodized)
- 4 tablespoons water
- Plastic spoon
- 2 tablespoons household ammonia
- Laundry bluing (can be found with laundry items in some grocery and hardware stores)
- Several pieces of porous material, like charcoal, brick, or stone
- Flat glass or ceramic dish
- Food coloring
- Waste Book

Stir the salt into the bowl of water and make sure that it dissolves completely or nearly as much as possible. Have an adult add ammonia and bluing to the bowl and mix everything together. Carefully pour the solution over the porous items in the dish. Thoroughly wash the mixing bowl.

Move the filled dish to a sheltered spot. Do not disturb! If you want some color in your garden, sprinkle a few drops of food coloring over the blue solution.

The next day, check to see what's happened. Are crystals starting to grow? Keep checking every day, and draw pictures of your observations in your Waste Book. In a week or two, your crystal garden will have bloomed all over the dish. Be careful—it's fragile!

The crystals that are growing in the dish are actually crystals of salt that you first mixed with the water. Ammonia helps the water to evaporate, and salt crystals latch onto tiny particles that are suspended in the bluing. The holes in the porous material actually draw the blue solution upward, a process called "capillary action." Capillary action encourages salt crystals to keep forming.

As a matter of fact, you can keep your garden growing for several more weeks by adding more of the water/salt/ammonia/bluing solution to the base of the dish.

Meredith Hollihan

Newton remained devoted to his mother for the rest of her life, and he spent long months in Woolsthorpe caring for her before she died when he was in his late thirties.

By 1670, Newton faced very real concerns about his religious beliefs. He was now an important figure at Trinity College. As with all professors at Trinity, he was expected to take holy orders by 1675 and become an ordained priest in the Church of England. Otherwise, he would have to give up his position as the Lucasian Chair of Mathematics.

Newton did not accept one of the major teachings of the Church of England. The Anglican Church, as with all Christian groups, recognized the doctrine of the Trinity. Growing up, Isaac Newton learned in church that God the Father, Jesus Christ, the son of God, and the Holy Spirit all were individual beings, yet all one and the same. "Three in One, and One in Three," is how a priest would explain one of the Church's greatest creeds. Christianity taught that Jesus was both the son of God as well as God Himself. Jesus, Christianity declared, was both a complete human being while still fully divine.

But as he grew older, Isaac Newton no longer could believe in the Trinity. He followed the ideas of an early monk in the Christian church named Arius, who had lived in Egypt in the 300s. Arians, named for this monk, believed that Jesus was indeed divine, but that he was entirely a separate being from God. To be an Arian, as Newton was, was to be a heretic, a traitor to the established Church.

Newton had to fight an inward, private battle. In his heart of hearts, he knew he could not go through a ceremony of ordination to become a priest. He could not swear on the Bible that he believed in the Trinity. But he could not reveal his true beliefs about the nature of Jesus. To do so would mean he would be excommunicated from the Church of England—thrown out of church and thrown out of Cambridge University. His good name would crumble, and he would never get another job in a university. Quietly, Newton began to hint that he might have to leave Trinity College.

Newton studied the Bible in search of arguments to back up his beliefs. He wrote out 12 statements in his notebook that explained his point of view, but he didn't reveal them to anyone else. Nowhere in the Bible is the Trinity mentioned, Newton wrote. The doctrine of the Trinity arose during a meeting of the early Christian Church leaders in the 320s. Newton explained that one side promoted the doctrine of the Trinity, while another group supported the Arian belief. A political dispute arose, and, ultimately, the group in favor of the Trinity took power

✤ The Trinity drawn as three faces in one Being.
Library of Congress LC-USZ62-50185

over the church. But to Isaac Newton, the Trinitarian doctrine was false teaching.

Somehow, Newton wiggled out of his problem. In August 1668, he made a trip to London and asked to be excused from becoming ordained—but to keep his job as Chair of Mathematics at Trinity College.

Newton had to make his request to no one less than King Charles II, the Supreme Head of the Church of England. King Charles granted his request, probably at the urging of Isaac Barrow, Newton's old professor, who now was an Anglican priest himself and an advisor to His Majesty. It seems likely that Newton never explained his true reasons to Barrow and made up some other excuse that Barrow accepted. However, the matter was settled. From that day forward, no one who ever held the Lucasian Chair was required to become a priest.

Isaac Newton was on a quest to open the mind of God. He continued to explore the Bible for signs and prophecies. He wanted to know the future. Newton eagerly read the prophets—the Book of Daniel in Hebrew texts and the Book of Revelation in the New Testament—looking for their predictions of future events. Christians taught that at the end of time, as humans experience it, God would return to establish a kingdom on Earth. So Newton looked to scriptures for clues predicting the time of God's return.

Newton also examined the floor plan of Solomon's Temple in ancient Jerusalem, the most holy shrine for Jewish believers. Newton revered King Solomon as one of the greatest figures among the ancients. Solomon designed the temple, Newton suspected, not only as a holy place but also as a secret guide to the future of every man and woman on Earth.

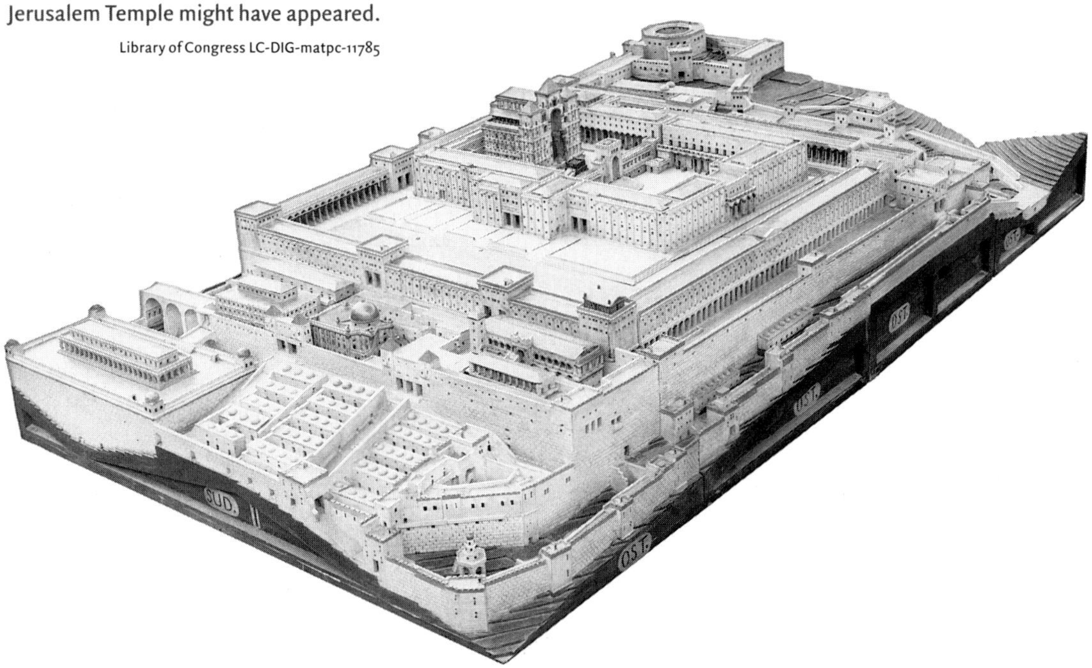

❖ An early model of how the Jerusalem Temple might have appeared.
Library of Congress LC-DIG-matpc-11785

A Mind Open and Shut

Barely anyone ever realized all that was going on in Isaac Newton's mind, or in his

Churches, Kings, and Freedom of Speech

Why did Newton and Galileo fear speaking freely about their beliefs? In their day, people who spoke against the government or the Church faced punishment and even death. Kings held power over their bodies, and the Church held power over their souls.

People, educated or not, lived in dread of what they could not understand. They feared witches who could work evil spells, as well as demons that possessed others. They believed that God sent fires, floods, and illness to punish wrongdoers. After someone died, God could deliver an even worse punishment: eternal damnation in the fires of hell.

Many freethinking people who spoke against their governments were executed by hanging like common criminals. Those who defied church doctrines, whether Roman Catholic, Lutheran, or Anglican, also faced death. Churchmen accused them of witchcraft and heresy and burned them at the stake to cleanse their souls. In the American colonies, as well, such beliefs were common. In Salem, Massachusetts, in 1692, 20 men and women were accused of witchcraft and hung or pressed to death with heavy stones.

Over centuries, democratic societies have made progress in how freely one may speak about political and religious beliefs. There are no more kings and queens in Europe with absolute power to punish people who oppose them. Church leaders do not imprison or burn people who question their teachings. In democracies around the world, traditions of religious and political tolerance have developed as free, open societies evolved, and democracies now believe that freedom of religious and political speech are basic human rights.

✤ In the 1640s, England's Puritan government arrested nonconformists who did not worship in the Puritan way.

A. A Witch . B A Spirit raised by the Witch
C. A Friar raising his Imps . D A Fairy Ring .
E. A Witch rideing on the Devill through the Aire .
F. An Inchanted Castle .

✤ A book "proving the existence of witches and spirits" was printed in London in 1684, the same year that Isaac Newton began to write *The Principia*.

Glasgow University Library, Special Collections Department

laboratory. Even those who lived in close quarters with Newton could not fully comprehend the depth of his studies. John Wickins copied hundreds of documents for Newton, but these did not deal with either alchemy or theology. Wickins never suspected that his chamber-fellow was a heretic. If he had, no doubt Wickins would have been horrified. Newton hid his work and beliefs well.

❖ Isaac Newton at the age of 46.

There was little that Wickins had to say about Newton at all. Once Wickins left Cambridge, he seemed to forget the small details of his life as Newton's friend. He left no memoirs of his Cambridge years. When Wickins' son asked about his father's years as Newton's roommate, all that Wickins recalled was Newton's "forgetfulness of food, when intent upon his studies" and that Newton could be pleasant in the morning if a night of work had resulted in an important discovery.

After Wickins left Cambridge, Newton needed a new assistant. He settled on young Humphrey Newton (not a relative), who came from the same school in Grantham that Newton had attended. For five years, Humphrey Newton worked at Isaac Newton's side. Unlike Wickins, Humphrey Newton left several letters that told of his boss's odd habits. After Isaac Newton's death, others interviewed Humphrey Newton as they prepared to write biographies about the mysterious scientist. All these documents shed valuable light on how intently Isaac Newton worked in his laboratory during those hidden years:

He very rarely went to Bed, till 2 or 3 of the clock, sometimes not till 5 or 6, lying about 4 or 5 hours, especailly at spring & ffall of the Leaf, at which Times he us'd to imploy about 6 weeks in his Elaboratory, the ffire scarcely going out either Night or Day, he siting up one Night, as I did another till he had finished his Chymical Experiments, in the Performances of which he was the most accurate, strict, exact: What his Aim might be, I was not able to penetrate into but his Paine, his Diligence at those sett times, made me think, he aim'd at somthing beyond the Reach of humane Art & Industry.

Clearly, Humphrey Newton had no clue that Isaac Newton practiced alchemy. Isaac Newton could work side-by-side with another person for years and never reveal his innermost thoughts. He could make a joyous discovery, or he could fall into deep depression. Either way, no one else knew. Humphrey Newton took care to note that he saw Isaac Newton laugh only once in the five years he served him.

Newton was not doing wizards' work, but by the time he was 30, anyone who saw him might have thought him one. Newton's hair, which he wore to his shoulders in the fashion of the day, was silver gray. Newton's mind, so open to new ideas, remained closed to people around him.

CHAPTER 7

SCIENCE'S MOST IMPORTANT BOOK

ON A BITTER January day in 1684, Robert Hooke, Christopher Wren, and Edmond Halley sat in lively conversation, likely in one of London's coffeehouses. Members of the Royal Society like Hooke, Wren, and Halley often gathered to swap stories and debate the issues of the day. This day, their topic was natural philosophy, specifically the nature of planets and their orbits. Why did planets circle the sun? What kept them from flying off wildly into space?

All three men believed that Johannes Kepler was correct in his thinking 150 years earlier. Planets, they agreed, travel around the sun in elliptical orbits. They also agreed that there is a principle, an inverse square law, which creates a hidden bond between the sun and planets. But Hooke, Halley, and Wren had a common problem: they had no way of proving their ideas. They couldn't do the math.

The story goes that Wren made an offer. Surely Isaac Newton would be able to offer an answer. Wren went on to promise a gift of a very expensive book to Hooke

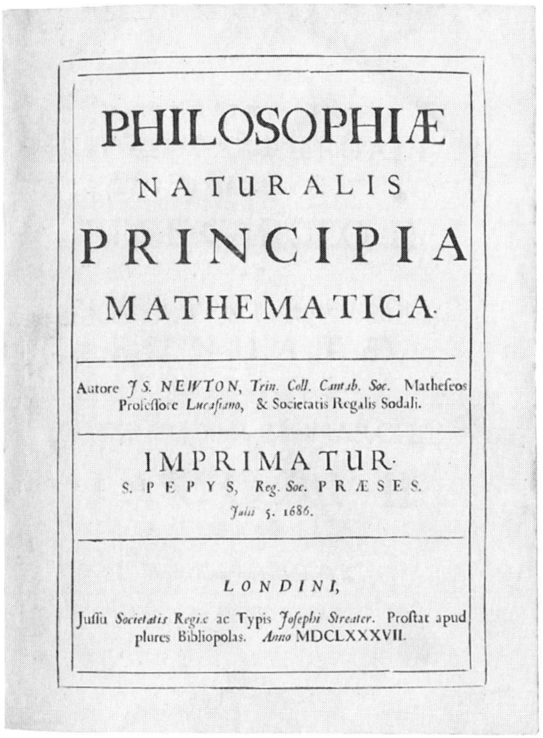

PHILOSOPHIÆ
NATURALIS
PRINCIPIA
MATHEMATICA.

Autore *J S. NEWTON*, *Trin. Coll. Cantab. Soc.* Matheseos Professore *Lucasiano*, & Societatis Regalis Sodali.

IMPRIMATUR.
S. PEPYS, *Reg. Soc.* PRÆSES.
Julii 5. 1686.

LONDINI,

Jussu *Societatis Regiæ* ac Typis *Josephi Streater*. Prostat apud plures Bibliopolas. *Anno* MDCLXXXVII.

✤ The title page of Isaac Newton's masterwork, the *Principia*.

and Halley. Whoever sought out and got a response from Isaac Newton would win the treasured volume.

Robert Hooke was not about to confront his archrival Newton in person. But seven months later, Halley did. In August, 1684, Halley showed up unannounced in Cambridge and made his query. Did Professor Newton have proof that planets journey in elliptical orbits?

To Halley's delight, Newton replied yes. Newton was certain about his answer. He had worked it out a good 10 years earlier, and had the proof on paper. But when the elusive Newton went looking for the proof, he apparently had second thoughts and claimed it was misplaced. Nonetheless, Newton sent Halley back to London with a promise to send him the proof as soon as he "found" it.

Three months later, the still untrusting Newton "uncovered" his paperwork. In November 1684, a nine-page paper, *De motu corporum in gyrum* (*On the Motion of Revolving Bodies*), reached Halley's hands. As he read the paper—in Latin, of course—Halley was astounded. Newton's explanation was a work of pure genius. Halley knew that somehow he must coax Newton into writing much more about his ideas.

During his visit to Cambridge earlier that year, Halley had taken a liking to the oddball Newton. It appeared that Newton liked Halley as well. But Halley had to wheedle Newton for some time until Newton finally responded to his pleas. Newton expanded those few pages of *De motu* into one of history's greatest books, the *Philosophiae naturalis principia mathematica* (*Mathematical Principles of Natural Philosophy*).

Once Newton began to write, he couldn't stop. Hidden away in his chambers at Cambridge, Newton dipped his quills into ink and scratched page after page of the *Principia* (prin-KIP-ee-uh). For over two years, he did nothing else. He sent the book a piece at a time to Halley, who excitedly awaited each arrival.

Halley the astronomer played a starring role by getting Newton's work into print. The Royal Society agreed to publish the *Principia* but provided no money for the project. The society had lost a bundle on its previous publication, *The History of Fishes*. Thus,

✤ Coffeehouse scene, c. 1700. Library of Congress LC-USZ62-47443

Edmond Halley and His Comet

Edmond (sometimes Edmund) Halley (HAL-ee) (1656–1742), the son of a soap maker, left Oxford University but became England's most famous astronomer.

Like Isaac Newton, Halley had a lively curiosity and was gifted at mathematics. As a student, Halley visited John Flamsteed, England's Astronomer Royal, at his observatory in Greenwich. Halley watched Flamsteed work at cataloging the stars and was hooked on astronomy.

✤ Edmond Halley was pictured on a cigar box.

The outgoing Halley had to draw Newton the recluse out of his shell. Halley charmed, encouraged, and downright buttered up Newton into writing the *Principia*. It was Halley, a mere clerk at the Royal Society with a family to support, who emptied his bank account to publish the *Principia*.

✤ Halley's Comet as it appeared in 1910.

Library of Congress LC-USZ62-89893

After Flamsteed died, Newton secured Halley a position as the new Astronomer Royal. Halley actually understood Newton's *Principia* and put Newton's math to work to learn how comets travel.

Until the early 1500s, people thought that comets traveled in straight lines. Newton and Halley felt that comets might be traveling in hyperbolas (great curves) or parabolas (tighter curves). In 1680 Halley looked back at ancient records. With just pen and paper, he created a huge database of 24 comets that had appeared over hundreds of years. Halley realized that the orbits of at least three actually were very long ellipses and not parabolas at all. Halley decided that the comets of 1531, 1607, and 1682 were one and the same.

Halley predicted that this comet would return to Earth 75 or 76 years after its appearance in 1682. Sure enough, in 1758, after Halley's death, the comet appeared. "Halley's Comet" (now "Comet Halley") has returned steadily ever since. It appeared in 1835, 1910, and 1986. Mark your calendar for its next swing by Earth in 2061.

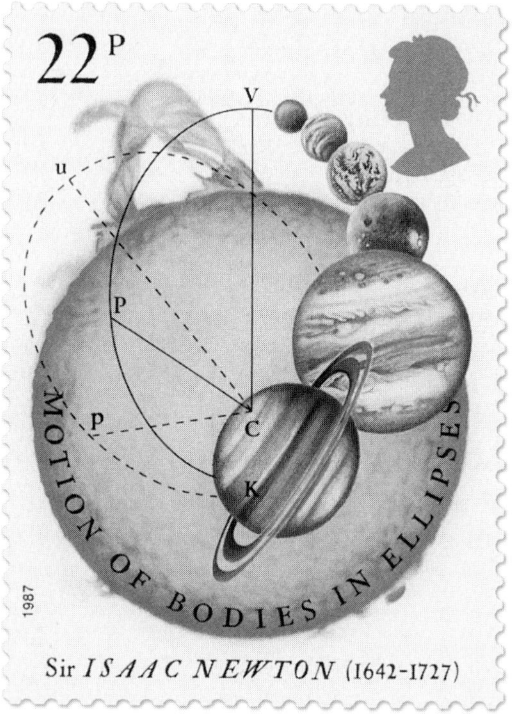

it fell to Halley to scrape up the pounds the project required. He risked going into debt when he footed the bill himself, but his gamble turned out to be a good one. When the *Principia* came into print, its reputation surpassed anything ever written about science.

Principles from Planets

In Newton's *Principia*, 20 years of observation, study, and thinking about the nature of all things came together. It took Newton hundreds of pages to roll out his thoughts. The *Principia* opened with a set of definitions that served as Newton's foundation for thinking about the natural world. In today's study of physics, these definitions still stand:

Matter—*anything that takes up space*

Mass—*the measure of a quantity or amount of matter*

Momentum—*the quantity of motion, which is the product of velocity (speed) and mass*

Inertia—*the power by which an object, if it is at rest, stays at rest, or if in motion, will travel in a straight line*

Force—*an action applied upon a body*

Centripetal Force—*an attraction toward the center of something (as in gravity)*

Once Newton had established these definitions, he laid out three laws that govern motion:

1. Law of Inertia. *An object in motion will stay in motion unless acted upon by an outside force. An object at rest stays at rest unless acted upon by an outside force.*

2. Law of Acceleration. *The rate at which the momentum of an object changes is proportional to the force acting on it.*

3. Law of Action and Reaction. *For every action, there is an equal and opposite reaction.*

As groundbreaking as Newton's Laws of Motion were, they served only as stepping stones to the biggest idea in the *Principia*: the Law of Universal Gravitation. When Isaac Newton looked at the night sky, he grasped that the earth, moon, planets, and stars all moved according to the same formula. Isaac Newton "got it"—"it" being gravity. In the *Principia*, Isaac Newton did the math to prove how gravity worked.

When Halley and his fellows in the Royal Society read the *Principia*, they were stunned. For the first time in Western science, someone was offering an explanation of universal gravitation, this mysterious force that held the universe together. The *Principia* threw

NEWTON'S FIRST LAW

IN ISAAC NEWTON'S day, people believed that an object moves because of its "impetus." For example, most people thought that when you throw a ball, the ball gains impetus that keeps it going until the impetus runs out and the ball falls to the ground.

Newton saw things differently. His First Law of Motion states:

An object at rest tends to stay at rest

and

An object in motion tends to stay in motion

Newton meant that any object that moves keeps on moving unless something else forces it to change its speed or direction. That also means that an object at rest, or not moving, stays still unless another force makes it move. We call this property of objects to resist changes in their state of motion "inertia" (in-ER-shuh).

You can do an experiment to demonstrate inertia using materials you have around the house.

YOU'LL NEED

- Sturdy paper (such as an index card)
- Table
- Quarter
- Dime
- Marble

Place the index card on the edge of a table so that the edge of the card extends beyond the tabletop. Put the quarter on top of the card.

Pull the index card quickly toward you. If you do this correctly, the quarter should stay on the table. Practice until you can make this happen.

Why does the quarter stay on the table?

The quarter has inertia, which keeps it in place as you pull the index card out from under it.

Try the activity again with a dime. Which coin has more inertia? Why? What gives an object more inertia?

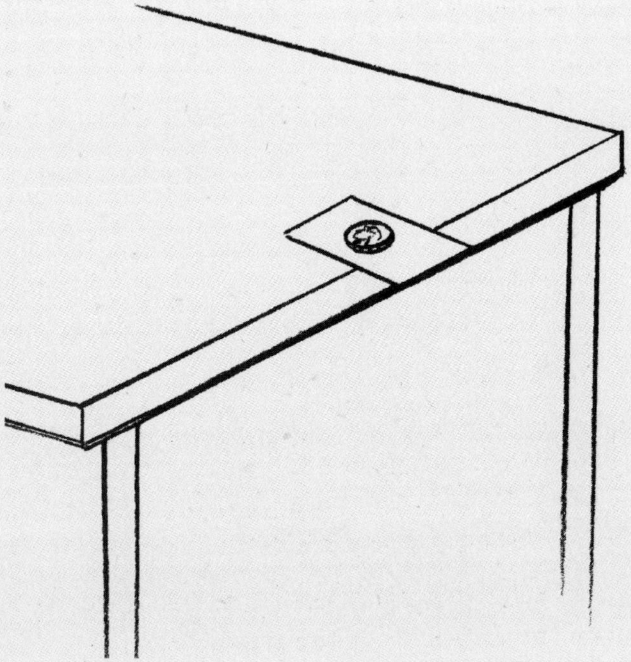

THINK: Have you ever watched a magician pull a cloth out from under an entire table that's set for dinner? What happens? Which of Newton's Laws is at work?

Now roll the marble down a long hallway. Eventually, it will stop rolling. Why?

Either your marble has rolled into another object, or friction from the floor has slowed it to a stop. Now roll the same marble down a carpeted hallway. Did it stop rolling sooner? Why?

THINK: What would have to happen to keep your marble rolling forever?

NEWTON'S SECOND LAW

NEWTON'S SECOND LAW of Motion builds on his First Law: If you apply a force to an object, it will move. This happens for two reasons:

The net force acting on the object

The mass of the object itself.

Force and mass work in relation to each other. The greater the mass of an object, the more force it takes to move it. Physicists put these rules into a simple formula:

Force = Mass × Acceleration.

Now you are ready to do the following experiment.

YOU'LL NEED

- Skateboard
- Several heavy items (such as large books or bricks)

Push the empty skateboard and watch it roll. Your push is creating net force; *you* are the only thing pushing the skateboard.

Now pile the books or bricks on your skateboard. Using the same amount of force you used before, push the skateboard again. What do you feel? Why? You are correct if you say that there is more mass with all the bricks on the skateboard—and it's harder for you to get things going.

Now change the amount of force you apply —push harder. What do you notice? How are force and mass related?

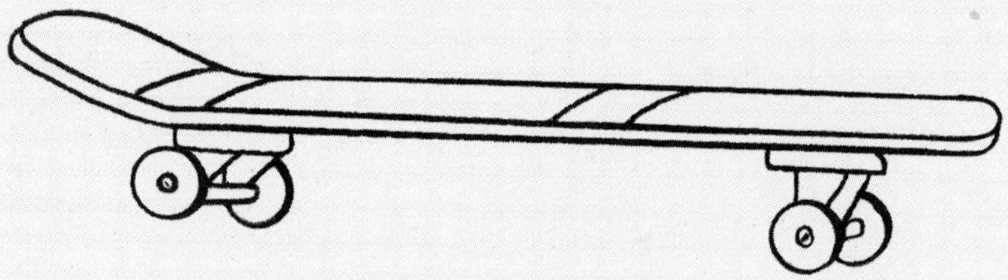

out 2,000 years of belief based on Aristotle's teaching that Earth operates by one set of rules while the sun, moon, planets, and stars follow different ones. Newton declared that a single set of rules governs everything we can see—and most likely things we cannot. Again, Newton's thinking showed that simplicity reigns.

The *Principia* marked the high point to Isaac Newton's original thinking about physics. Over the next 20 years, he would refine and revise his masterwork into three volumes. He showed that laws of gravity and motion work at great distances. He proposed that the same laws extended to objects so small human eyes cannot see them. But in the 1680s, Newton had no lenses strong enough to test this idea for himself.

Newton never went forward with new research into the workings of the universe. After publication of the *Principia*, his life took a different path.

Gravity: The System of the World

To today's students, Newton's Laws of Motion are familiar and may seem easy to understand. But many educated people in 1687 still had medieval notions. They believed that planets and stars moved under their own power. They had no concept of gravity. They did not understand that "what goes up must come down." Nor could they grasp how objects in outer space follow the same laws that keep our feet planted firmly on Earth.

Scientists today call Newton's view of things the "mechanistic universe." Descartes had also suggested that the universe operates like a giant machine, but Newton disagreed

NEWTON'S THIRD LAW

OF NEWTON'S THREE laws of motion, his Third Law is most familiar:

> **For every action, there is an opposite and equal reaction.**

Let's say you blow up a balloon and let it go. You already know what will happen: the balloon will zoom around the room. But... what is the *action* that is taking place? And what is the *reaction?*

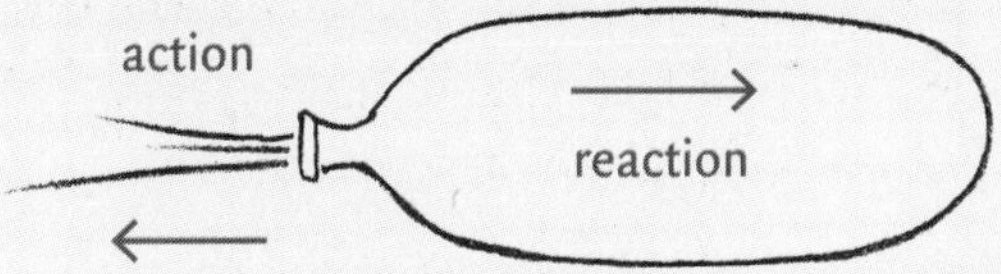

Notice the action and reaction take place at the same time.

What will happen if your balloon is inside something else? Give it a try. Build a boat and watch Newton's Third Law in motion.

YOU'LL NEED

- Half-gallon milk carton
- Cellophane or masking tape
- Nail
- Balloon
- Clothespin, chip bag clip, or alligator clip
- Bathtub or pool

Cut the milk carton in half lengthwise so that you have a boat about two inches tall. Use the tape to shape the front and back of your boat so that the edges are smooth.

Use the nail to punch a small hole in the middle of the stern (end) of your boat. This will serve as the "exhaust pipe" of your new creation.

Blow up the balloon and push the end through the "exhaust pipe" hole from the inside out. Clamp the balloon shut with the clothespin or clip.

You're ready to launch! Set the boat on the surface of the water and let the clip go.

What happens? How far does your boat go? What can you do to make it go faster or farther? Where is the action? The reaction?

Just for fun, thread the end of the balloon through the hole from back to front. What happens then?

You might want to make other boats using other kinds of containers. Why does your boat work best when the bow (front) is pointed?

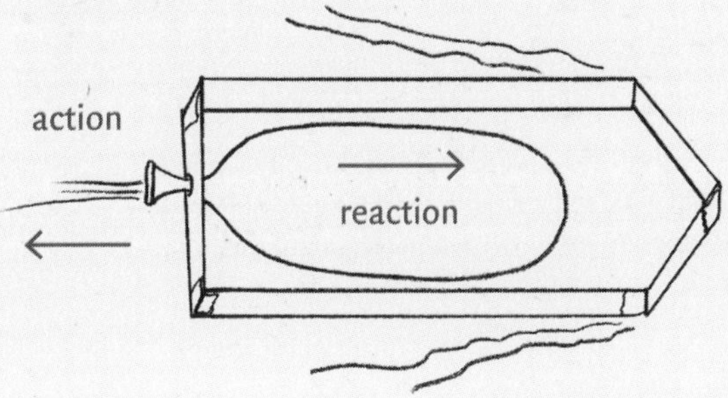

with Descartes' claim that planets travel in whirlpools of vortices. Newton wrote that gravity, not vortices, makes all objects—large and small, near and far—cooperate in machine-like perfection.

Newton compared the universe to the mechanism of a huge clock. Clocks work in ways that can be measured and counted. Newton declared that gravity makes the universe work in the same manner. Gravity works far out in space in exactly the same way it works on Earth. Isaac Newton had developed the theory of universal gravitation.

Newton used the moon as the example for his claims about gravity. The moon was simple to observe, its orbit easy to track every 28 days. He applied his laws of motion to the moon's orbit in this way:

> *The moon is always falling down toward the earth (Law of Gravity)*
>
> but
>
> *The moon is always traveling in a straight line due to inertia (First Law of Motion)*
>
> therefore
>
> *The moon follows an orbit around the earth.*

Just as he had with optics, Newton used experiments to test his ideas about gravity. The *Principia* devoted much space to these explanations, but the book was nearly impossible to understand. Except for a handful, even the most learned members of the Royal Society could not begin to grasp its ideas. Back in Cambridge, as Newton took a walk on the street one day, one student was heard to tell another, "There goes the man that has writt a book that neither he nor any body else understands."

When Newton was an old man, he offered a simpler story to a dinner guest about how he came upon the idea of gravity. It all happened, Newton recalled, when he was a

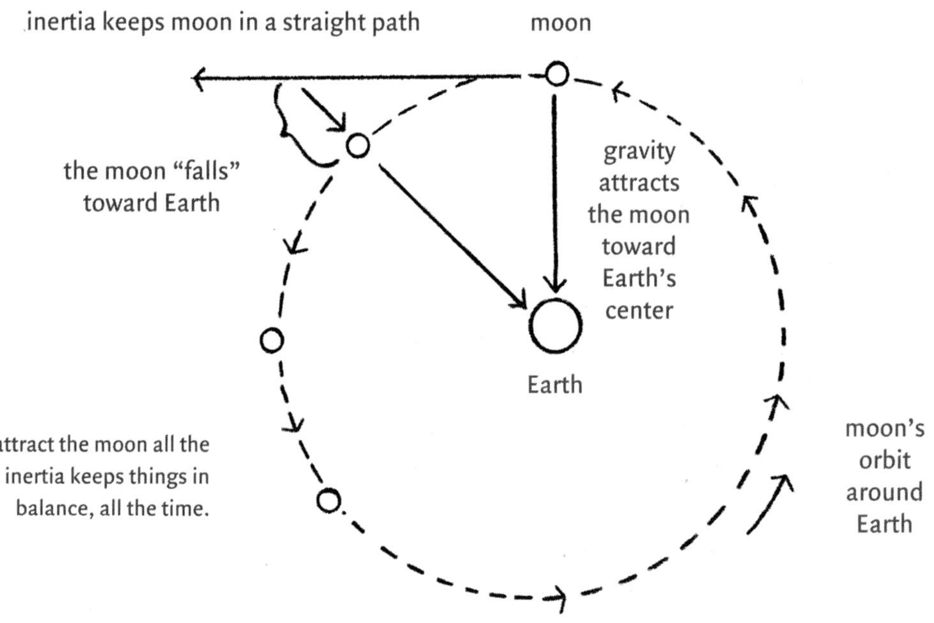

✤ Gravity could attract the moon all the way to Earth, but inertia keeps things in balance, all the time.

young man hiding from the plague at home in Woolsthorpe.

Newton explained his discovery. Outdoors, he had watched an apple fall from a tree to the ground. As always, the apple fell *down*. Newton sensed that whatever pulled the apple downward also pulls the moon toward the earth. The apple was much closer, so the earth's pull was much stronger on the apple than on the faraway moon. But apple or moon, the earth exerted a force on each. Newton called this force "gravity."

Newton tested his thinking about gravity like this:

1. He knew the apple had fallen just 16 feet from the tree to the ground.

2. He knew how far it is from the ground to the earth's center.

3. He also knew how far the moon is from the earth's center—60 times farther than the apple tree was.

But only one law must apply to both. And that, Newton declared, would be the inverse square law:

Force = $\frac{1}{d^2}$ *("d" stands for distance)*

Thus, Newton calculated, Earth's gravitational pull on the apple is 60^2—60 × 60—or 3,600 times stronger than its pull on the moon.

Newton well might have made up his tale about gravity to amuse his guest. Tall tale or not, the notion of an apple falling toward the center of the earth offered his guest a clear picture of how gravity works.

In the *Principia*, Newton applied his ideas about gravity to other natural events such as the paths of comets. This notion excited astronomers like Flamsteed and Halley, who used Newton's mathematics to predict the return of a giant comet that had swept through the skies in 1680. Newton also used his calculations to show how the moon's gravity tugs at the earth to create the rise and fall of tides on oceans everywhere.

By the 1700s, during the Enlightenment, better instruments allowed natural philosophers to make enormous progress in scientific discoveries. They were able to test Newton's ideas and confirm that Newton was correct.

Then, in the early 1900s, an unknown patent clerk named Albert Einstein put forth his own ideas about the nature of the universe. Einstein asked about what happens to objects as they travel near the speed of light. Einstein also asked about the motion of particles that are smaller than atoms and molecules. Unlike the natural philosophers of Newton's

times, physicists in the later 1900s had the benefit of instruments to test Einstein's ideas for themselves.

Like Newton's ideas, Einstein's theories shook the world. But even to this day, no one has found a way to fully explain gravity.

Thinking About Force

In school, you have no doubt learned about various kinds of forces—gravity, friction, magnetism, and so on—all observable forces. Newton's work dealt with things he could observe with the instruments he had available to him in the 1600s. Sometimes Newton did "thought experiments" in his head. In the next few pages, you can think about forces and do a few simple physical and mental exercises to help you understand them.

Feel the Force

Forces are simply the constant pushing or pulling on things everywhere. Hook one end of a rubber band to a stationary object, such as a knob on a closed door. Pull on the other end of the rubber band.

It might seem that your right arm is doing all the pulling, but the rubber band is pulling back, too. A force can feel like a pull, but it can feel like a push, as well. And that continuous push/pull tells us another fact about force: forces always work in pairs. If a soccer goalie blocks a ball with his chest, the goalie is pushing the ball away.

Gravity

Did you ever watch a baby sit in a highchair and drop things to the floor? You might get annoyed at having to pick them up, but for the baby, the process is fascinating. No matter what that baby pushes off the tray, objects always fall down.

Sure, you say, that's because gravity pulls them in that direction. Remember though, there are *two* forces at play. For instance, are you holding this book up as you sit at a desk? The book would fall down onto the desktop, but your hands are pulling it up. Are you slouched back in your chair? If the back of the chair didn't push you up, you'd fall over backward.

A similar process occurs when you stand on the earth. Your body pulls the earth toward you and the earth pulls back, although you cannot feel this at all. Why not? Let's say that you weigh 100 pounds. A 100-pound mass of *you* is pulling on the earth. However, the *entire mass of the earth* is pulling on you, always and all at once. In other words, Earth's gravity is the force that pulls you down. But at the same time, your body makes its own tiny tug to pull the earth toward you.

How Does "Mass" Differ from "Weight?"

MASS is the amount of matter in an object. More specifically, mass is the measurement that describes how much an object resists being moved. The greater the mass of something, the more difficult it is to move from its position when it's standing still.

Still don't get the picture? Think back to the previous section. Picture you, a 100-pound kid, pushing against the earth with your bare hands. It's *you* pushing *your force* against the earth, whose mass is roughly 6×10^{21} metric tons. That's your mass, 100 pounds, against the earth's mass, 6,000,000,000,000,000,000,000 tons. In numerals, this would read "6 sextillion tons." (If you are expressing things in pounds, make that about 1.32×10^{25} pounds.)

Here's a common mistake many students make. We measure mass in pounds or kilograms. So you might think that mass is the same thing as weight. But that's not so. *Weight* describes how much gravity is pulling on you. On the earth, if you weigh 100 pounds, it means that Earth's gravity is pulling 100 pounds of you toward the earth's center. On the moon, though, you would weigh only one-sixth as much, or about 16 pounds, even though your mass is the same.

Yes, the moon has gravity, too, but the moon's mass is only one-sixth the mass of the earth, with one-sixth as much gravitational pull. However, your mass is the same whether you are on the earth or on the moon. If you sat on a sled on either the earth or the moon, it would take just as much force to get you moving—no matter whether you're sledding on snow or moon dust!

Friction

As objects move, lots of things resist them. We call this "friction." Solids, liquids, gases—all three states of matter cause friction when something moves against them or through them.

Wave your hands through the air. You can feel air molecules push against your palms. Rub your hands together. Friction from both palms makes your skin heat up. Clap your hands. Friction works there, too, as you smash more air molecules between your hands.

Air, water, other objects, and the earth itself all cause friction to resist a body in motion. Do you remember the story that Galileo dropped lead balls off the Leaning Tower of Pisa? Do a thought experiment. Imagine that you drop your loaded backpack and a single sheet of paper off a roof at the same time. You are correct if you think your backpack will hit the ground first. Why? Air resistance will catch the paper and cause the paper to float on its way down. The same thing won't happen with your heavy backpack. As the backpack travels this short distance, there is not enough friction to push back on your backpack to slow down its fall to the ground.

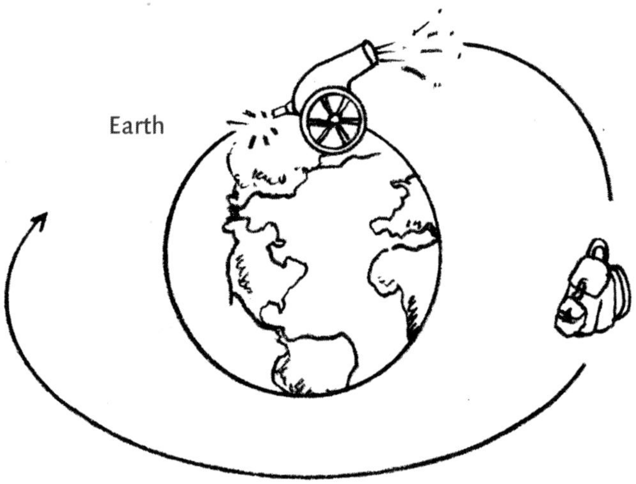

But imagine that you could drop your backpack from a skyscraper one mile high. As the backpack starts to fall, it moves faster and faster until it reaches terminal (maximum) velocity. But the air is pushing back against your backpack. Your pack keeps falling but cannot fall any faster. The air pushes back and causes drag on your backpack.

Try another thought experiment. Suppose you decide to launch your backpack into orbit. What's required? You are right if you think that you'd need a rocket or some kind of really huge cannon. You find the world's biggest cannon and load your backpack. What would it take for your backpack to make it into orbit? Look at the question another way. What's resisting your backpack as it flies toward space?

In order for your backpack to escape Earth's atmosphere, your cannon must force it beyond the pull of Earth's gravity. That means your cannon must fire a monumental blast to force your backpack into space. (In actual terms, your backpack must travel at least seven miles per *second* in order to escape Earth's pull on it.) Your backpack must travel exceedingly fast with incredible force. Too fast, and your backpack will escape all together and fly off into space. Not fast enough, and it will fall to the ground.

If you launch your backpack at just the right speed, Earth's gravity will capture it and send it into orbit. For a time, your backpack will circle the earth. Eventually, though, friction from other things like solar wind particles and other objects in orbit will cause your backpack to lose speed, and it will fall back to Earth.

Forces on the Moon—and Everywhere Else

Now imagine that you are standing atop a building on the moon with your backpack and a piece of paper. On the moon there is a vacuum—no air at all. If you drop your backpack and paper off the roof, they will hit the moon's surface at exactly the same time. There is no air on the moon to create friction to slow the paper down.

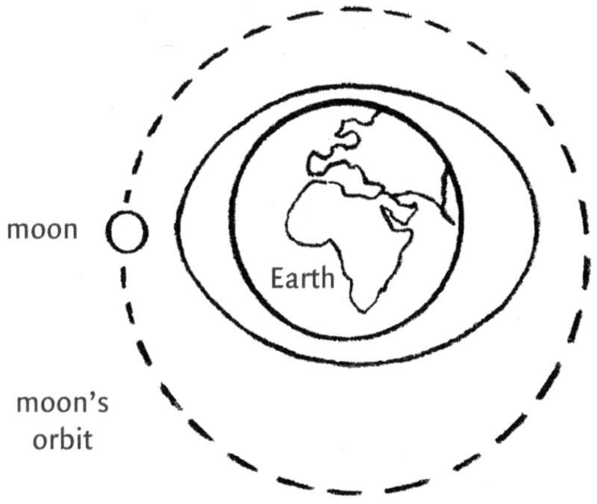

Yes, the moon doesn't have air, but it certainly has gravity. Can you think how the moon's gravity might affect things here on Earth? (If you answered "tides," you are correct!) As the moon orbits the earth, it tugs at the earth's oceans and pulls them up away from land. The tide usually rises and falls twice each day. As the moon circles the earth, it pulls not only the ocean but also the earth's crust and core, so that the ocean rises on the opposite side of the earth, too.

On December 22, 1968, astronauts on the U.S. Apollo 8 mission circled the moon and took the first view of an "Earthrise" from beyond our nearest neighbor in space. NASA

St James's Square
Germain (Jermyn) Street
St James's
Park
Tower Hill
Tower of London
St Georges Fields
Artillary Ground
Smith field
LAMBETH
Churches on Southwark side.

CHAPTER 8

LOOKING FOR CHANGE

On February 6, 1685, Isaac Newton could hear the church bells in Cambridge sound a slow, deep toll. Serious news had arrived from London. The king was dead, and he had no heir to take his Crown. Charles II, the "Merry Monarch," had plenty of illegitimate sons and daughters by his long string of lady friends, but the king and his wife, Queen Catherine, never produced a child of their own.

The masters of Cambridge frowned in worry. Charles's younger brother James would take England's throne, and James was an ardent Catholic. Cambridge University was strictly a place for members of the Church of England. The university's leaders were deeply suspicious of Roman Catholics, whom they accused of "popery"—holding their allegiance to the pope in Rome.

James was crowned King James II, and immediately the new king set out to solidify the position of the Catholic Church in England. His actions were nothing new; ever since the days of Henry VII, the Church of England and Roman Catholics had battled for control of the monarchy, if not the soul of England herself. All through the land, James and his supporters installed Catholics as leaders in government and in churches. James did the same thing with universities. In early 1687 he charged a university leader in Cambridge with misconduct and tried to install one of his own followers.

✤ A map of London in the late 1600s shows Germain Street (Jermyn Street), where Newton lived, and the Tower of London, where he worked at the Royal Mint.

Isaac Newton took part in the uproar that followed. Though Newton secretly questioned the Church's beliefs about the Trinity, he firmly stood with the Church of England against popery. Newton joined Cambridge officials who used their pens and wits to fight back against King James's attempts to bring Catholicism to Cambridge University.

✽ (ABOVE) King James II (1633–1701) (RIGHT) William of Orange was welcomed to England during the Glorious Revolution.

Newton joined a group of Cambridge officials who traveled to the Royal Court in London to stand up for their position against one of the King's most dangerous judges, Lord Jeffreys. Lord Jeffreys's name was on the tongue of many Englishmen because he had ordered the hanging of 320 peasants who rebelled against King James.

Despite supporters like Judge Jeffreys, the inexperienced King James met strong opposition when he tried to impose Catholicism on England. Then James found himself in even more trouble. In November, 1688, a Protestant hero from Holland, Prince William of Orange, set sail with Dutch warships for England. In Cambridge, 50 miles from London, Isaac Newton guessed correctly that the Dutch had won a victory. As the story went:

> ... *their guns were heard as far as Cambridg, and the cause was well known, but the event was only cognisable* [clear] *to Sir Isaac's sagacity* [wisdom], *who boldly pronounc'd that they had beaten us ... by carefully attending to the sound,* [Sir Isaac] *found it grew louder & louder, consequently came nearer. from whence he rightly infer'd* [figured out] *that the Dutch were victors.*

James's power base crumbled, and he fled to Catholic France where he could live safely. By now, Isaac Newton's name was well

POWER TO THE PARABOLA

ISAAC NEWTON'S REFLECTING telescope caught the eye of everyone at the Royal Society because of its unique design. Instead of just magnifying objects in space, Newton's little scope used a concave mirror to capture light and reflect it to a mirror that bounced the image into an eyepiece. Newton harnessed the power of the parabola—the same shape as a concave mirror—in the very same way the Hubble telescope works today in deep space.

You can do a different kind of experiment to discover the power of the parabola for yourself. Build a parabolic oven. "Catch" some light—and heat—and use them to roast marshmallows! This experiment works best on a sunny day.

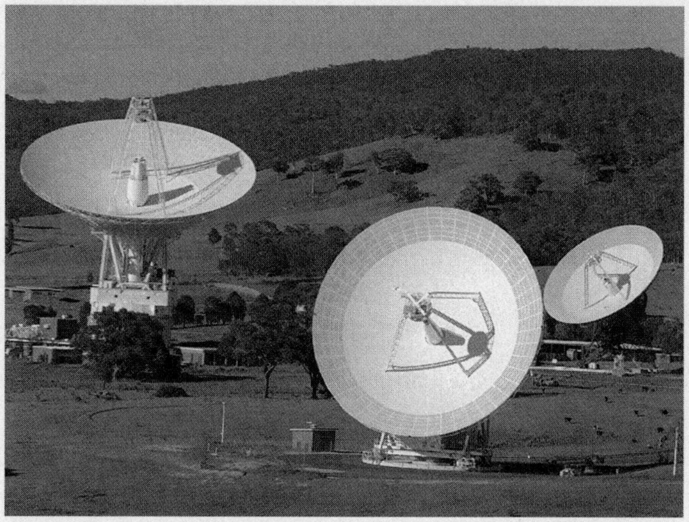

❖ The Canberra Deep Space Communications Complex, located in Australia, uses satellite dishes to capture signals from deep space. NASA

Adult supervision required

YOU'LL NEED

- Plain paper
- Pencil
- Scissors
- Glue stick
- Paper plate
- Aluminum foil
- Masking tape
- Marshmallows

Fold a piece of paper in half lengthwise. Then unfold it and place the paper so that the fold matches the straight line of the pattern on the following page. Trace the pattern, making dark, solid lines from the outside edge toward the dotted circle in the middle. Trace this half-circle using dotted lines. Then turn the paper around and trace again. Cut out the pattern around the outside edge only.

Now it's time to glue. "Sandwich" the pattern, the paper plate, and the foil together using a glue stick. Glue the pattern on the outside of the plate and glue the foil on the inside. Make sure that the glue covers every surface.

Once it is dry, use the paper pattern as a guide to cut around the outside of your "sandwich" in a circle. Then cut along the solid lines toward the center. Do not cut past the dotted line that circles the center!

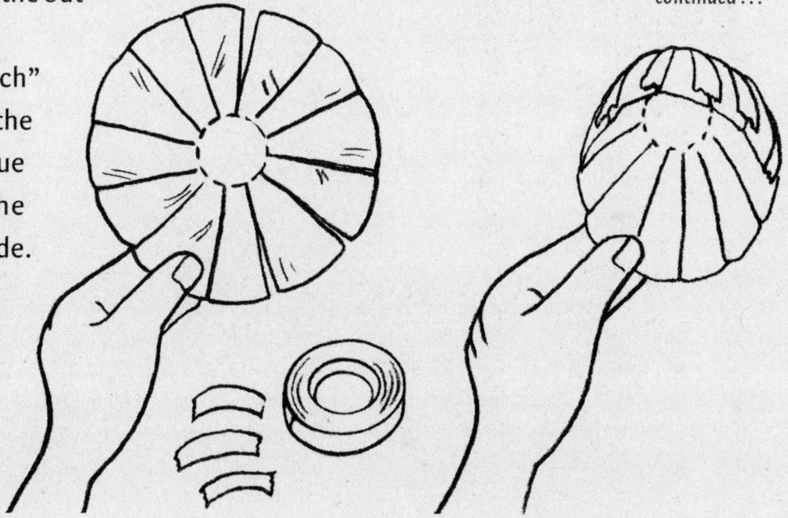

You're ready to build your oven. Cut 11 pieces of tape so they'll be handy when you need them. Then pick up the oven and overlap each wedge so that the edge is about halfway across the one next to it. Use the tape on the back of the oven to hold each wedge in place. You want the oven to stand up in a shape that's a little bit like a satellite dish, only deeper.

Your oven is not a perfect parabola like a satellite dish, but it can "catch" sunshine quite well.

continued . . .

POWER TO THE PARABOLA *continued*

NOW FOR THE FUN PART: Place your parabolic oven in the sunshine, put a marshmallow inside, and point it directly at the sun. Watch what happens, but be careful: this little oven can cook that marshmallow hot enough to burn your fingers!

Why do you think your oven does a good job of roasting marshmallows? What would happen if you just put foil on a flat paper plate and tried this experiment? Now extend your thinking a bit: Why was Isaac Newton's reflecting telescope such a success?

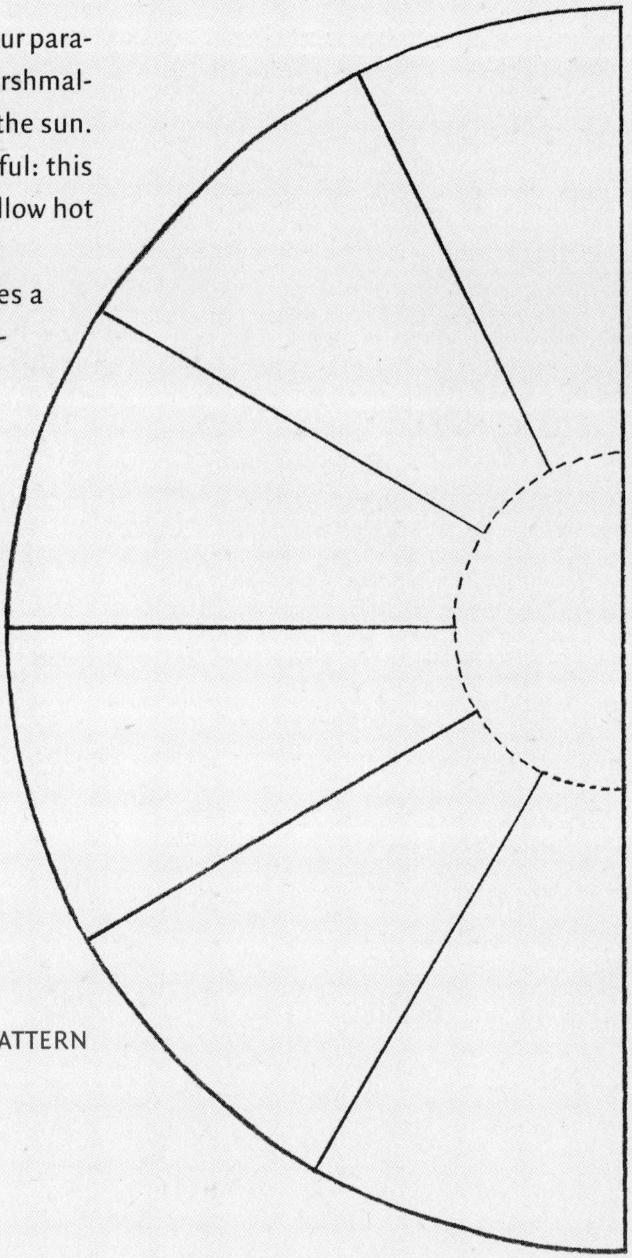

PARABOLA PATTERN

known at Cambridge, and Cambridge's freemen elected him as their representative to the English Parliament. Newton began his duties in 1689 as Parliament struggled to find a new candidate to take the empty throne. Ultimately, Newton and the others decided that the best choice would be the Protestant Princess Mary, James II's daughter by his first wife. Princess Mary's husband was the popular Prince William of Orange. In 1690 the pair was crowned in England's historical church, Westminster Abbey in London, as co-rulers William and Mary. Isaac Newton probably witnessed the many parades and processions that marked England's Glorious Revolution and its new rulers' rise to one of Europe's great monarchies.

London held other attractions for Newton, and he began to travel back and forth from Cambridge. The release of the *Principia* opened Newton's thinking to all sorts of learned people, not just natural philosophers. As the *Principia* brought Newton's thinking about gravity and motion to public acclaim, it brought fame to its author in equal measure. Newton met with Christiaan Huygens several times to swap ideas about light, colors, and motion. For the first time, he became more interested in his social life and began to make serious, if sometimes awkward, friendships.

The respected philosopher John Locke sought Newton out, and the pair became friends. As brilliant as Locke was, he could never claim to understand the mathematics in the *Principia*. However, he saw that Newton's written explanations of his science were pure genius.

Newton, who had never willingly shared his insights with others, treated Locke differently. For years they corresponded about all of Newton's interests except for mathematics, a topic where Newton far outpaced his illustrious pen pal. A favorite issue in their letters was religion. Apparently comfortable that his friend shared his opinions about the nature of God, Newton revealed in his letters his true thinking about the Trinity. Such frankness was a big departure from Newton's usual secrecy.

Newton also became a friend of Samuel Pepys (PEEPS), a Londoner who invited Newton to dine at his home. Like Newton, Pepys was a Cambridge man, respected as the president of the Royal Society. Pepys enjoyed an active social life. He had an energetic curiosity about the world and surrounded himself with men and women who could either entertain or inform him. For more than 10 years, Pepys kept a diary to chronicle not only his exploits—he had many adventures—but also the tiniest details of his days.

In 1687 Newton made the acquaintance of a gifted mathematician newly arrived from Switzerland. His name was Nicolas Fatio de Duillier (FAH-tyo duh DWEE-yay), a young man whose head was filled with the teachings of Descartes. Quickly Newton set the youthful scholar straight in his thinking, and Fatio, as he was called, readily accepted Newton's principles to explain gravity and motion. Newton became Fatio's mentor, and Fatio became Newton's adoring pupil.

As with John Wickins, Newton's friend at Cambridge, Newton seemingly developed an all-consuming attachment to Fatio. They visited back and forth in London and Cambridge, and Fatio often carried letters from Newton to Christiaan Huygens and Gottfried Leibniz on the European mainland. The friendship between Newton and Fatio ended due to some misunderstanding that has never become clear. Fatio left England. As promising as his career had been, he never achieved the greatness that Newton could have predicted for him.

As Newton spent more and more time in London, life in the capital city grew ever more appealing to him. It became clear to him that London, and not Cambridge, was the seat of intellectual fever in England. In the quiet away in Cambridge, he had been able to think great thoughts and accomplish

✤ "William and Mary"—King William III (1650–1702) and Queen Mary II (1662–1694)

Samuel Pepys

When Isaac Newton became a friend of Samuel Pepys, neither one knew that Pepys, who had a secret, would become one of England's most significant writers.

For 10 years, from 1660 to 1669, Pepys kept a private diary. He recorded small details of his everyday life, the friends he visited in taverns and coffeehouses, who came to dine, and how he got along with his wife Elizabeth, whom he married when she was 15 and he was 22.

Pepys was an English civil servant, a government employee who spent his long career in the Office of the Admiralty that controlled England's navy. However, Pepys had plenty of time away from work. Like King Charles II, Pepys loved to party. His diary offers colorful details about London during the Restoration.

Samuel Pepys (1633–1703)

Pepys knew the cast of characters who flocked around the flashy king, and he gossiped about them in his diary. He attended concerts and kept company with famous actresses. Pepys actually survived an operation to remove a large kidney stone—centuries before patients had anesthesia or doctors washed their hands before operations.

Today we would call Pepys an "armchair scientist." His interests spanned all kinds of natural philosophy including chemistry, biology, and astronomy. When he was 30 and working for the Admiralty, Pepys hired an English sailor to teach him the math used to measure timber and build ships. Pepys became president of the Royal Society and helped to bring forth Newton's *Principia* for publication. His name is on the title page.

Pepys made his journal entries in code, using the same kind of shorthand writing that Newton learned at school. In his diary Pepys told of taking down, word for word, King Charles's story of how he escaped from his enemies during the English Civil War. He also recorded his eyewitness account of how the Great Fire of London burned the city to the ground in 1666.

his research. But only in London could Newton connect with powerful men at the Royal Society who could publish his work and communicate it to the rest of Europe.

Driven to Depression

After the *Principia* appeared in 1686, Newton buried himself in revising it and fine-tuning the text. As Newton worked, his fame grew as fast as the waxing moon. He must have felt uncomfortable about his growing reputation as men from London wanted to meet with him to get answers to their questions and letters arrived from overseas. As flattering as this attention was—and there is every sign that Newton liked to be flattered—he was at heart a shy and awkward man.

As Newton thought about whether to move to London, he realized he would need a job to support himself in the lifestyle of a city dweller. A man of his social standing would need a house and servants, typical of his friends like Pepys and Locke. But finding a suitable position in London wasn't easy. Newton was not well-connected with anyone who could give him letters of introduction into London's social network.

The process of looking for a position stretched on for several years, and sometime

WHAT ARE THE ODDS?

IN 1693 ISAAC Newton's friend Samuel Pepys wrote Newton a letter with an urgent request. Pepys had made a bet on a game of throwing dice, and he wanted to know if he was going to win it.

Here is Pepys's question:

If Player A throws six dice and at least one 6 turns up, he wins. If Player B throws 12 dice and at least two 6s turn up, he wins. If Player C throws 18 dice and at least three 6s turn up, he wins. Which player is more likely to win?

Isaac Newton said, "Player A." Pepys did not believe him. But Newton was correct—and he had several different ways to explain. Newton based his answer on a branch of mathematics called "probability" (the chance that something will *probably* happen).

You can roll dice, chart your results, and see how probability works, as well. To simplify things, you will use only three dice. The more times you roll the dice, the more mathematically precise your results will be.

You can do this activity by yourself, but it's fun to have a partner help you. You will throw one die, while your partner will throw two dice at once. (When you have only one of a pair of dice, it's called a "die.")

YOU'LL NEED

- Waste Book
- 3 dice
- Partner

In your Waste Book, make a chart that looks like this:

PROBABILITY MATCH UP

How many times does one throw turn up a 6?

Player A	**Player B**
Throw one die	Throw two dice
Record a "win" if you roll a 6	Record a "win" if you roll two 6s
1 ________	**1** ________
2 ________	**2** ________
3 ________	**3** ________
4 ________	**4** ________
5 ________	**5** ________
6 ________	**6** ________
7 ________	**7** ________
...	...
24 ________	**24** ________
25 ________	**25** ________
Total Wins ______	**Total Wins** ______

NOW IT'S TIME TO PLAY: Player A throws one die. If a 6 turns up, record it as a win under Player A's column on your chart. Player A keeps rolling one die and records results 25 times. Player B throws two dice. If 6s turn up on *both dice*, record a win under Player B's column on your chart. Like Player A, Player B must roll all the dice 25 times.

Sometimes both players might win; sometimes both might lose.

Now add up the number of wins rolled by Player A and Player B. Whose total is higher? If your results follow Newton's way of thinking, then Player A should have more wins than Player B.

According to probability, there is a greater chance of Player A rolling 6s than Player B rolling double 6s. Player A has a 1 in 6 chance of rolling a 6 when throwing one die. Player B has only a 1 in 36 chance that two 6s will turn up on a roll of two dice.

Probability deals with what will *likely* happen. However, Player B might actually roll more wins than Player A. One way to find out if the odds went against Player A is to keep on rolling the dice. If you play long enough, eventually Player A will roll more wins than Player B.

Take your thinking a little further. What if you were rolling three dice at one time?

A Straight Shot at Playing Around with Forces

HAVE YOU EVER played in the yard with a bucket of water and swung it around or over your head? At first, the water sloshes around in the bucket, but as you swing faster, not a drop spills out. There are two forces at play here. Your hand and arm act as centripetal force that pulls the bucket inward, toward you. A second force, inertia, tries to keep the bucket (and water inside it) moving in a straight line. When you swing the bucket just fast enough, you bring the forces into balance, and the water stays in the bucket.

What would happen if you let go?

You can watch the same forces at work using a Ping-Pong ball and a piece of string.

Adult supervision required

YOU'LL NEED

- Ping-Pong ball
- Tool sharp enough to poke holes in the ball or pry it open
- Fishing line or kite string
- Tape

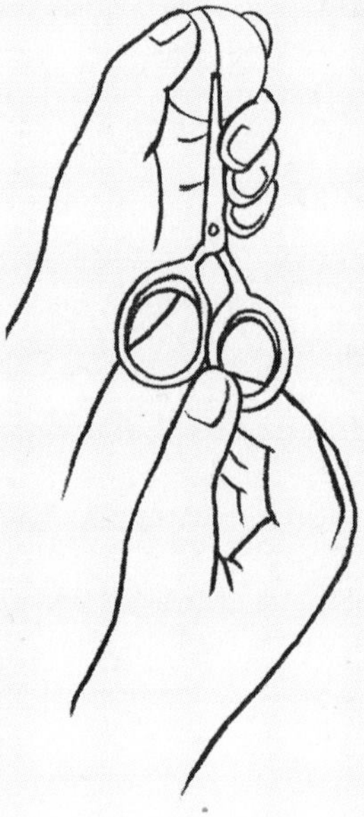

Have your adult helper pop two holes on opposite sides of a Ping-Pong ball along the seam. Make them just large enough so that the string will slide through but still "grab" the ball, and then knot one end. (You might need to tape the seam shut in a place or two.)

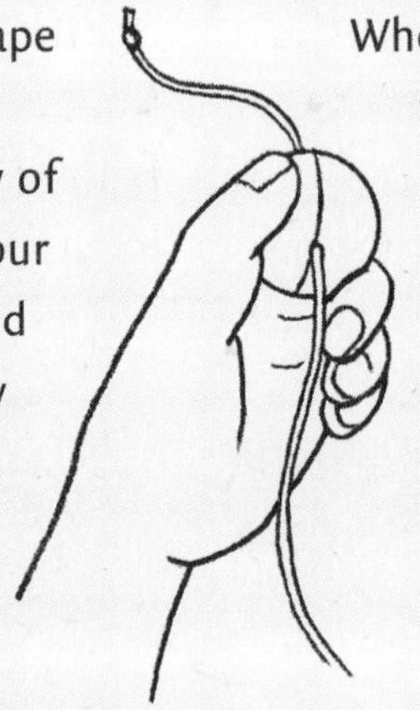

Go outside where you have plenty of room. Take someone along to act as your observer. Hold the string at the loose end with the Ping-Pong ball about halfway down the string. Start to swing the string and ball over your head. What happens to the ball? (It slides to the end of the string.) Can you guess why? (Your hand and arm create centripetal force that pulls the string straight. According to the law of inertia, the ball wants to go straight.)

Swing the string and ball over your head so they are going at a good speed. Then let the string go. Where does the ball fly? (The ball should fly off in a straight line.)

Here's another principle you can observe. The faster you twirl the ball, the farther it will fly when you let go of it. That just makes sense, right? Now think about what would happen if you had a baseball attached to the end of the string. How much more effort would you need to get the ball into orbit by twirling it around your head? (You would need to work much harder.) Then, what would happen when you let go? (The ball would fly much farther.) The more force you apply, the farther the ball will fly.

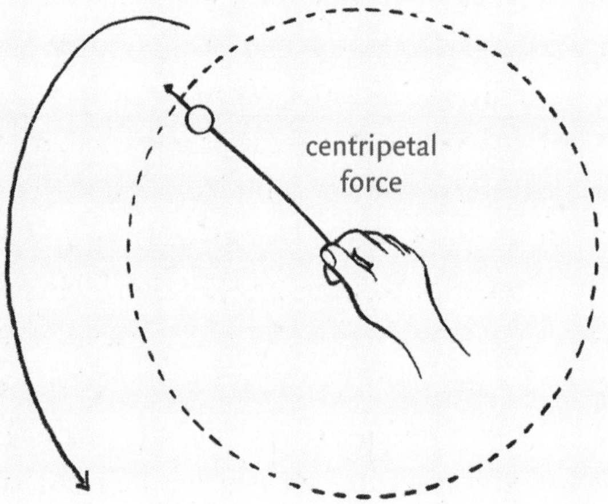

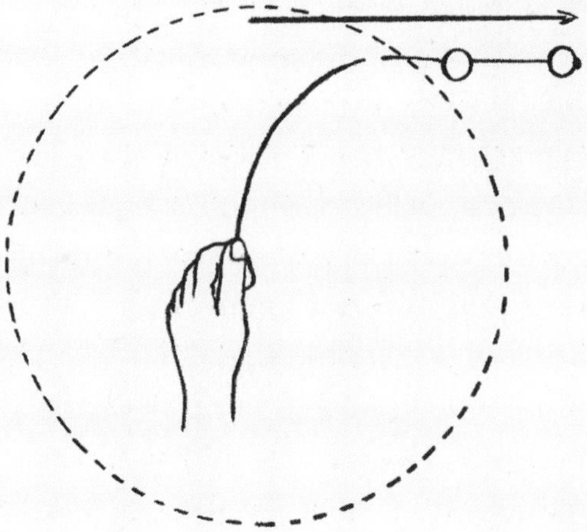

during the first half of 1693, 51-year-old Newton fell into a deep depression. It was as though he had dropped into a black hole. From his chambers in Trinity College, he wrote angrily to his good friends Locke and Pepys. Newton's letters were wildly off-balance. To Pepys he wrote, "I am extremely troubled about the embroilment I am in... but am now sensible that I must withdraw from your acquaintance, and see neither you nor the rest of my friends anymore...."

Newton furiously scrawled that Locke had tried to "embroil me with woemen [women]" whom Newton probably felt were a distraction from a life devoted to serious study and thought. For several months, he had no official contact with anyone outside a small circle of people in Cambridge.

People wondered what happened. Rumors spread that Newton collapsed after a fire in his rooms destroyed some of his work on the revision of the *Principia*. Others thought that, after all the flurry of getting the *Principia* into print, Newton was simply worn out. Twenty exhausting years of secret work in alchemy had gone nowhere. Newton's break with Fatio de Duillier and the loss of his young admirer could have added to Newton's troubles. Even the strain of going public with so many well-known scientists and scholars, together with the worry he felt about finding work in London, could have pushed Newton past the breaking point.

But by mid-September 1693, Newton's London friends began to get brighter letters from him. Newton offered an explanation for his strange acts:

> *The last winter by sleeping too often by my fire I got an ill habit of sleeping and a distemper wch this summer has been epidemical put me further out of order, so that when I wrote to you I had not slept an hour a night for a fortnight* [two weeks] *together and for 5 nights together not a wink.*

Signs showed that Newton was beginning to recover from his breakdown. He began to revise the *Principia* in order to answer the questions of those who had read it. Again he took up writing letters to mathematicians such as Gottfried Leibniz. He renewed his ties with his friends in the Royal Society, such as Locke and Wren.

As he made additions and changes to the *Principia*, Newton fine-tuned his own thinking about the nature of matter and of motion. Newton was an "atomist." He believed that tiny particles of matter were scattered throughout a universe that is mostly empty space. Gold, he wrote, is made up of particles within particles, proven by the fact that both mercury and acids can penetrate it.

✤ Isaac Newton as a middle-aged man.
Library of Congress LC-USZ62-10191

✤ A rival mathematician referred to Newton as a lion known by "the mark of his claw."

When he applied this thinking to giant bodies such as planets, Newton argued that the same rules were in place. Space, he said, is mostly empty, and gravity keeps the planets and comets in their regular orbits. "...since all phenomena of the heavens and of the sea acting in accordance with the laws described by me; and since nature is very simple, I have myself concluded that other causes are to be rejected and that the heavens are to be stripped as far as may be of all matter...."

As the 1690s wore on, Newton also continued to work on other topics like mathematics and optics that had consumed him when he was a young man. But now he was more than one-half century old himself. The creative part of his life in scientific research was complete.

But one afternoon in 1697, Newton returned home tired from a busy day to find a challenge waiting for him. An unnamed scholar had published a very tough math problem and challenged others to solve it. Newton sat down immediately, took pen in hand, and wrote the correct answer. The challenger later declared that no one but the great Isaac Newton could have provided the solution: "We know the lion by the mark of his claw."

By now, all of Newton's angling for a position in London was starting to pay off. At Trinity College, Newton had befriended a young gentleman named Charles Montague. The fortunate Montague was a well-to-do student whose father paid his way through Cambridge, and Montague never had to prove himself as a scholar. However, as an adult, Montague wanted so much to read the *Principia* he paid for extra math lessons in order to understand what Newton wrote in his masterpiece.

After Montague left Cambridge, Newton kept track of his friend's progress. Montague held a position in the Royal Mint, the part of England's treasury that manufactured coins. As Montague took ever-more important jobs, his influence grew. By 1694, he was Chancellor of the Exchequer (similar to the post of Secretary of the Treasury in the United States). Newton was well aware of his young friend's growing power and made sure to stay connected to him.

With Montague's help, Isaac Newton, at the age of 53, became warden of the mint in 1696. As with everything he did, Newton attacked the duties of his new job head-on. He left Cambridge University and Trinity College, and except for one brief visit, he never returned. He looked forward to a new life in London. All that Isaac Newton needed to do was to master the mint.

CHAPTER

9

A MAN OF LONDON TOWN

THE ROYAL MINT stood securely within the walls of the Tower of London, England's most famous fortress. The castle, already 600 years old when Newton was alive, sat surrounded by a moat and two thick stone walls. It was a perfect spot to house a factory that made coins of the realm in precious gold and silver crowns, half-crowns, guineas, farthings, and pennies.

As warden of the mint, Newton found that his hands-on job meant he not only had to work in the tower; he had to live there, as well. The back of his small home shared the tower's outside wall and faced the wall of the inner "keep." His quarters were not luxurious. For all practical purposes, Newton was living in a factory that operated 20 hours a day.

From four o'clock in the morning until midnight, six days a week, the mint turned out coins. Teams of horses pulled wooden cranks in endless circles to power giant machines that rolled coin metal into thin sheets. Pairs of men then used hand-operated presses to "strike" coins of all sorts. The noise deafened anyone nearby, and the stink of hot metal floated throughout the grounds where Newton worked and lived.

Moreover, the tower also housed the Ordnance, the office of the government responsible for equipping the English army and navy with weapons and supplies for war.

Newton cared little for the soldiers posted there, and general rivalry between the mint employees and the soldiers annoyed him. In just a few months, the noise and confusion overwhelmed Newton. He abandoned the warden house at the wall and moved to Jermyn Street in Westminster, an upcoming London borough.

Newton came to work each day as the mint was in the midst of a huge change. The treasury was in search of old coins so that it could transform them into new ones. The coins that jingled in English subjects' pockets and purses dated back as far as the days of Queen Elizabeth I, who had died nearly a century earlier. Over time, the coins took a beating as they passed back and forth between the hands of merchants, aristocrats, and common folk. Coins also were "clipped" by unscrupulous people who took tiny bits off the

✤ (BELOW) The Tower of London Library of Congress
(RIGHT) Workers struck "coynes" (coins) at the Royal Mint. Royal Mint

edges, melted them down, and sold the scrap silver and gold as though it belonged to them. Counterfeiters, some of them master forgers, created fake coins that looked like the real thing. People could not be sure that the money they accepted for goods they sold or services they performed actually came from the Royal Mint.

England was plagued with counterfeiting at the time. Counterfeiters made impressive profits by reselling England's very wealth as their own. England's economy was based on the amount of silver and gold the small nation held in its treasury, which included all of the country's coins. Even tiny bits of precious metal lost to counterfeiters added up over time to major losses.

"Coyning" (manufacturing fake money) frustrated officials at the highest levels of government. Phony coins devalued real ones. Counterfeiting did serious damage to England's wealth, and therefore, to England's security among its rival nations like France, Holland, and Spain. King William was in Europe fighting a war for England. The English did not want more trouble at home with their own citizens trying to steal from the Crown.

Isaac Newton seized onto his job as warden with his usual single-minded passion. He set about researching the mint's history, which extended far back to the days of King Edward IV in 1465. Newton hand-copied page after page of documents that were hundreds of years old. With his mathematician's skill at organization, he put to rights all the recordkeeping that was so vital to the mint's well-being.

Newton also took the mint's manufacturing process to task. He made careful studies of every step in the process, performing the role of "efficiency expert." Thanks to his oversight, the process was running far more smoothly just two years later. Then in 1699, the master of the mint fell ill and died. There was little problem in replacing him—

❉ In the late 1900s, the Bank of England printed Isaac Newton's portrait and reflecting telescope on the back side of the one-pound note, the currency of the United Kingdom.

✤ By the time Isaac Newton sat for this portrait, fashionable Englishmen cut their hair short and wore elaborate wigs.

Newton's thoroughness guaranteed that he knew how the mint operated. Newton had mastered his job, and now he moved from serving as warden to becoming master of the mint.

England's leaders had decided that counterfeiting money was an offense of treason. They reasoned that counterfeiters were just the same as spies or traitors who sold secrets to enemy governments. Beginning in 1697, condemned counterfeiters faced the same horrible form of execution that was used to punish spies or revolutionaries. They were to be "drawn and quartered"—hung until not quite dead, disemboweled, and cut into pieces.

The English government gave Isaac Newton the duty of building evidence against these counterfeiters. Newton found this order a distasteful one, and his letters show that he tried to direct this task toward another branch of the government. His superiors ignored his request and even gave him a clerk to help. The job of convicting counterfeiters was just too important, and Isaac Newton was their man to get that job done.

Just as he had gotten the milling of coins into good order, so did Newton hunt down the men and women who counterfeited. He put on the clothes that common people wore and hung out in taverns to spy on counterfeiters. He made trips to London's Newgate prison, where he took down the stories of inmates, poor men and women who clipped and "coyned" for the bigger thieves who employed them.

But it was not just poor people who counterfeited money. Newton followed the trail of one William Chaloner, a crook who dressed like a gentleman. Chaloner, highly skilled at running an operation in fake coins, enjoyed "funning" (cheating) the English government. He managed to buy off witnesses against him even as he sat in prison. He lied every which way he could about his fellow criminals in order to save his own neck. When that didn't work, he tried to charm his way out of trouble.

Eventually, however, Newton helped the government to build an airtight case against Chaloner, and a court convicted him. Chaloner wrote an emotional letter to Newton, begging to be spared from his murder at the hands of the English government. Newton actually had no control over Chaloner's fate, and Chaloner died as a traitor, drawn and quartered.

The Royal Society Reemerges

Even as he labored at the Royal Mint, Newton kept up with his interests in natural philosophy and his meetings at the Royal Society. His position as master of the mint paid him 500 pounds each year—a tidy sum compared to the few pounds his mother had given him when he was a struggling sizar at Cambridge University. In 1702 Newton decided to leave Parliament as its representative from Cambridge University. Newton cut his last ties to Cambridge. He had other plans in mind.

In 1703 Robert Hooke died. Newton's old enemy at the Royal Society was gone forever. In a series of half-hearted votes, members elected Newton as president. Christopher Wren had been nominated for the job, but he passed it up. Newton, Wren thought, was the better scientist.

As much as he had despised Hooke, Newton built on his old enemy's practices as curator of experiments at the Royal Society. During the Society's most productive years, meetings were filled with exciting, worthwhile discussions about science and mathematics. Hooke's job was to arrange for members to view each other's experiments and share one another's research papers. However, as Hooke grew older, the society took on leaders who were not scientists. Meetings spiraled downward into discussions about freaks of nature and how people poisoned each other.

✤ Isaac Newton was commemorated on a two-pound coin issued by the Royal Mint. Inscribed on the side of the coin is the phrase "Standing on the Shoulders of Giants."

Isaac Newton recognized that the Royal Society was heading downhill and set matters straight by making its meetings more professional. To some extent, his efforts succeeded. Members returned, and the topics for discussion reached a higher level. But even the illustrious Dr. Newton could not keep his members from sharing some tidbit or other of a bizarre discovery. One day, Newton found himself presiding over a discussion about four dead piglets found "all Growing to One Another." Not until the 1800s did the Royal Society finally establish itself as a leader in scientific discussion and inquiry, a reputation that holds true today.

In 1705 Isaac Newton journeyed to Cambridge for one last reason, to add a title to

✤ Queen Anne (1665–1714)

Christopher Wren

Isaac Newton aside, the most famous member of the Royal Society was Sir Christopher Wren. Wren was a gifted mathematician, astronomer, and architect.

Like Isaac Newton, Wren liked to build little machines and models when he was a boy. He attended Oxford University, and by the time he was 25, he was chairman of astronomy at a London college. But after Wren returned from a visit to Paris, he looked at buildings with a fresh eye for design.

In August 1666, a fire in a bakery on London's Pudding Lane blazed into fury. Londoners already were at their wits' end fighting the plague that had struck two years in a row. Now 100,000 people were homeless. Wren and his friend Robert Hooke worked to rebuild England's capital in a grand style. As a new London arose from the ashes, many of its buildings incorporated his style.

In the 1670s, Wren and Hooke designed the Monument, a 202-foot-tall pillar. For 300 years, onlookers assumed that it was a memorial to the Great Fire. However, in the early 2000s, a historian visited the Monument and found a long-abandoned room below ground. Hooke and Wren had designed the Monument to serve as a science laboratory. From the top to bottom, this pillar was designed for experiments that needed heights. Moreover, the pillar, when fitted with lenses, could serve as a telescope.

Wren is entombed in his masterpiece, St. Paul's Cathedral. An inscription on the wall nearby reads:

Beneath lies buried the founder of this church and city, Christopher Wren, who lived more then 90 years, not for himself but for the public good. Reader, if you seek his monument, look around you.

✤ Sir Christopher Wren (1632–1723) Library of Congress LC-B2-5234-10

✤ (ABOVE) St. Paul's Cathedral (RIGHT) Tomb of Sir Christopher Wren in St. Paul's Cathedral, London.

✤ Londoners camp out as the Great Fire burns.

✤ The Monument served a double purpose.

his name. Queen Mary's sister Queen Anne, who now held the throne, visited the university and honored Newton by making him a knight, "Sir Isaac" Newton.

Playing Politics with the Royal Society

NEWTON wasted no time in building his own empire in the Royal Society. He artfully used his presidency to promote his own standing among natural philosophers. Several times, he abused his power and dealt with others unfairly. In particular, he wielded his authority to lord over John Flamsteed, the king's astronomer.

For decades, Flamsteed worked from his observatory at Greenwich to build huge catalogs, records of data that tracked the motion of the moon, planets, and stars through the heavens. Flamsteed's intellectual gifts came nowhere near those of Isaac Newton, but his records were vast and accurate.

In the 1690s, Newton had trouble with his calculations about the motion of the moon, and he needed Flamsteed's observations for his own research. Flamsteed was as picky about his paperwork as he was about his star charts. For years, Flamsteed held off Newton's request. He wanted to finish his catalog of the stars and present all of his observations at once in one magnificent volume, *Historia britannica coelestis* (*British History of the Heavens*). Flamsteed's cantankerous personality could be as annoying to Newton as Newton's own behavior was to others, and the two became enemies.

For 20 years, Newton and Flamsteed played cat and mouse. However, the "cat" grew into a lion; as president of the Royal

✤ John Flamsteed (1646–1719)

✤ A series of stamps issued in the United Kingdom show the history of astronomy, including Isaac Newton's accomplishments.

Society, Newton used his power to rob Flamsteed of the papers that he had finished up to that point. Then Newton made sure that the Royal Society published only part of them, the part that *Newton* thought was important.

Not to be outdone, Flamsteed stubbornly continued to chart the night sky and record his observations. He published his complete version, *Historia coelestis*, in 1712. Four years later, a twist of fate put most of the copies of the work that Newton had pirated back into Flamsteed's possession. With great pleasure, Flamsteed burned them. Newton could never get his hands on them again.

Flamsteed died in 1716. Nine years later, two of Flamsteed's loyal assistants published an even better version of the *Historia coelestis*, which stands as the most authentic edition of the work that took Flamsteed an entire lifetime to accomplish.

✤ Isaac Newton's living room, adorned by his portrait on the end wall. Babson College Archives

Rooms in Red

As a man of wealth and influence, Isaac Newton needed a woman to run his household and act as a hostess to visitors. Newton had no wife, and so he brought his half-niece, a Miss Catherine Barton, to London from the countryside in 1696.

Unlike her peculiar uncle, Catherine Barton sparkled with charm. Her looks, intelligence, and magnetic personality proved to be a huge draw to a large circle of men. It was not long before Catherine's name floated in the gossip among Londoners in coffeehouses and gentlemen's clubs, where adoring fans toasted her with special glasses engraved with her name.

Rumors began to circulate that Miss Barton had moved into the home of Charles

Bake an Apple Pye in a Coffin

APPLE "PYE" (PIE) has been a much-loved treat for people in Europe since the Middle Ages. A housewife baked her pies in a "coffin"—a tough pastry container. In earlier years, people didn't eat the coffin; they simply enjoyed the filling. However, by the time Isaac Newton was a boy, people were eating pie, coffin and all. This poem by William King shows that apple pie was a favorite treat during Newton's lifetime:

> Of all the delicates which Britons try
> To please the palate of delight the eye,
> Of all the sev'ral kings of sumptuous far,
> There is none that can with applepie compare

A cook in Isaac Newton's house might have made her apple pie using a recipe like this:

> To make pyes of grene apples
>
> Take your apples and pare them cleane and core them as ye wyll a Quince, then make youre coffyn after this maner, take a lyttle to fayre water and half a dyche [dish] of butter and a little Saffron, and sette all this upon a chafyngdyshe [chafing dish] tyll it be hoate then temper your flower with this sayd licuor [liquid], and the whyte of two egges and also make your coffyn and ceason your apples with Sinemone [cinnamon], Gynger and Suger ynoughe. Then putte them into your coffin and laye halfe a dyshe of butter above them and so close your coffin, and so bake them.

You can bake a modern version of this old favorite using "grene" Granny Smith apples. To save time, make the coffin using a prepared piecrust that you buy from the grocery store dairy case.

Adult supervision required

YOU'LL NEED

- Oven
- Potato peeler
- 6 large Granny Smith apples
- Knife
- Bowl
- 1 cup white sugar
- ¼ cup flour
- 1 teaspoon ground cinnamon
- 1 teaspoon ground ginger
- Spoon
- 2 ready-made pie crusts
- 9-inch pie pan or square pan
- 2 tablespoons butter, cut into small peices
- Foil strips

Preheat the oven to 425° F. Core and peel the apples, cut them into wedges about ¼ inch thick, and place them in the bowl. Sprinkle the apples with sugar, flour, cinnamon, and ginger. Use a large spoon to "toss" the mixture so that the apples are well coated. Set aside.

Following the directions on the crust package, remove the pie crusts. Lay one crust in the bottom of the pan so that it follows the pan's shape. If your pan is square, you might need to fit the crust a bit; if you tear the crust, patch it together with your fingers. There should be some extra crust hanging over the edge of the pan.

Layer the apple mixture into the pan so that the apples are close together. Then take the pieces of butter and lay them all over the top of the apples. Place the second crust upside down over the apples. Then use your fingers to pinch the edges together all around your pie.

Use the knife to cut short slits in the crust so steam from the pie can escape as it bakes. Put foil strips around the edge of your pie so the crust does not bake too quickly.

Have an adult help you place your pie in the middle of your oven. Watch it carefully to make sure it does not burn. After 30 minutes, remove the foil strips from the crust.

foil strip

It will take 40 to 50 minutes altogether for your pie to bake. The crust should be golden brown, and juice will bubble out of the slits. Set it on a rack to cool. Enjoy!

CREATE CLUES IN A PORTRAIT

CONTEMPORARY PEOPLE MOSTLY rely on photographs when they want a formal portrait of themselves. But when Isaac Newton became famous, he had to call an artist to his home to paint his likeness. The better known Newton became, the more often a new portrait appeared.

Portraits hold clues about their subjects' nationality, place in society, religion, families, and even their pets. In Newton's time, anyone looking at a portrait would know to look for these clues.

For example, study the portraits of King Charles II and his archenemy Oliver Cromwell. Both were created at about the same time in the 1600s. Both men ruled England, but their portraits offer clues about why they differed so much. Look carefully at them. What do their details tell you? (You can find some answers below . . . printed upside down.) Take a look at the other portraits in this book. Do they hold clues, as well?

✤ Oliver Cromwell

✤ King Charles II

YOU'LL NEED

- Art supplies (you choose, see instructions below)

Make a portrait of yourself or someone you know. You can use paint or markers on paper, model with clay, or make a collage using objects you find. Plan your project before you start. What kinds of symbols will you use to give clues about your subject?

Clues to Portraits of King Charles II and Oliver Cromwell:

1. Both Charles and Cromwell wear armor, because both were military leaders. However, Charles's armor is more decorative, and his fancy shirt and flowing hair show that he is a Royalist. Cromwell's clothing reflects his Puritan roots and that he lived a stricter life.
2. King Charles is pictured with his Crown, while Cromwell, who though he was England's Lord Protector, refused to be king or wear a Crown. The boats show that Cromwell built up England's navy.
3. King Charles did not have a legitimate son who could follow him on the throne of England. Cromwell did have a son named Richard who followed him as England's leader, but he soon fell from power.

Montague, Newton's patron at the Royal Mint, without marrying him—an enormous scandal. Montague's older brother had died, and Newton's friend had inherited the title and estate from his dead father. Now he was a powerful aristocrat, Baron Halifax. Vicious gossip accused Newton of setting up his niece with his influential friend as a way to thank him for past favors. Possibly Catherine Barton and Charles Montague were secretly married. Historians have never been able to determine the exact truth.

In any case, Catherine Barton publicly took a husband in 1717, a much younger man named John Conduitt. Sometimes they lived with Newton in Leicester (LES-ter) House, a stone building on a fashionable street in Westminster, where Newton had moved in 1710.

Isaac Newton was a man of means, and he needed a home worthy of his standing as England's leading scientist, president of the Royal Society, and master of the mint. Catherine Barton Conduitt decked out Newton's home in crimson red trappings of all sorts. No one is sure why, but red covered everything—sofas, chairs, and draperies in the room where he entertained visitors, and the bedspread, pillows, and small couch in the chamber where he slept. Perhaps Catherine Barton chose red to echo the color of her uncle's gowns as a professor at Trinity College. Certainly it was a color fit for a gentleman of Newton's fame.

Catherine's new husband sought Newton's company, and Newton took a liking to him. An amateur scientist and member of the Royal Society, Conduitt was both smart and curious. The pair spent long hours together, with Newton spinning tales of his childhood and years as a student at Cambridge. Newton loved to talk about his adventures in natural philosophy, and Conduitt wrote them down. John Conduitt holds credit for documenting the legendary tale of Newton and the falling apple.

After Newton's death, Conduitt planned to write a long biography about his uncle-by-marriage, but Conduitt himself died just 10 years later. The biography he had planned survives only as a set of rough drafts. Even so, Conduitt interviewed many people who knew Newton as a young man in Woolsthorpe, Grantham, and Cambridge. Thanks to his work, we have a wonderful peek into the early life of a complicated man.

Other visitors to Leicester House wrote about its master's amusing, if strange, ways. Even as a rich old man, Isaac Newton was still so lost in his own thinking that he got mixed up in his daily routines. William Stukeley, an "antiquary" who wrote about the history of

Lucky to Learn

As you read this book, have you noticed that every member of the Royal Society was a man? Unless she was Queen, a woman of Isaac Newton's day did not take part in public life—not in government, education, or in the Church.

"A learned woman is thought to be a comet, that bodes mischief whenever it appears," complained a scholarly woman. Women were thought to be physically weaker than men, with weaker minds. It was important that they not overtax their brains with study.

A girl's chance at an education depended on what her father thought of the idea. In wealthy households, a girl might learn to read and write along with her brothers and their tutors, but when the boys left home for university, she stayed behind. In any case, a girl was educated to manage her household, read the Bible, and see to her sons' learning. Isaac Newton's mother, Hannah Newton Smith, could write only a little—a perfect example.

A few women of the upper class wrote novels, autobiographies, and histories. At the height of his fame, Newton met the Princess of Wales, Princess Caroline, a serious student who collected books and built a remarkable library. Curious about Newton's study of the Bible, she often called on him to visit her at court.

Émilie, Marquise du Châtelet (mar-KEES doo shat-uh-LAY) was a French countess educated in mathematics and languages. She became a friend and mistress to Voltaire, France's foremost intellectual, who admired Newton's work.

Madame du Châtelet translated the entire *Principia* into French. No one has written a French translation of the *Principia* since. In 1749 she died after giving birth.

✤ Princess Caroline is greeted by her husband, the Prince of Wales, the future King George II.

the times, wrote about his visit to Newton. The story appeared in an old book:

> *Dr. Stukeley called one day by appointment. The servant who opened the door said that Sir Isaac was in his study. No one was permitted to disturb him there; but, as it was near his dinner-time, the visitor sat down to wait for him. In a short time a boiled chicken under a cover was brought in for dinner. An hour passed, and Sir Isaac did not appear. The doctor then ate the fowl, and, covering up the empty dish, desired the servant to get another dressed for his master. Before that was ready, the great man came down. He apologised for his delay, and added, "Give me but leave to take my short dinner, and I shall be at your service. I am fatigued and faint." Saying this, he lifted up the cover, and without emotion, turned about to Stukeley with a smile, "See," he said, "what we studious people are! I forgot that I had dined."*

That day, Stukeley saw for himself why Newton's servants had gossiped about him for years.

CHAPTER

THE LION'S ROAR FADES AWAY

WITH A HEALTHY income of £500 per year as master of the mint and secure as president of the Royal Society, Sir Isaac Newton's high-standing position in London society was guaranteed. Newton seemed to put his secret ways behind him when he moved to London. Now he took great pleasure in the "society" of others. A wealth of visitors flowed in and out of his Westminster home. High-ranking Londoners, other fellows from the Royal Society, and natural philosophers from overseas all came to call on the great man.

Of course, a series of half-nieces and nephews stayed in touch with him too. Newton had outlived his half-brothers and sisters, and their children always were happy to have the attention of their famous—and rich—Uncle Isaac. On occasion, he traveled to Woolsthorpe to check on his estate, still a sheep farm that also produced an income for him. Newton was generous with his family and made them gifts of money before he died. In fact, anyone named Newton in the whole of England thought it perfectly fine to ask Sir Isaac for money. Many times, he actually helped them.

During his later years, Sir Isaac solidified his earlier work in natural philosophy. With Robert Hooke no longer around to fault his ideas, Newton brought out the first English edition of *Opticks* in 1704. A Latin version followed in 1706, and an English

❉ Portraits of Isaac Newton show him as a well-off gentleman (ABOVE) and at work in his study (ABOVE RIGHT).

revision in 1717. Newton also published several books of mathematics, again polishing work that he had completed decades earlier in Cambridge.

In 1709, at the mature age of 66, Newton started revising the *Principia*, and it appeared in 1713. A third edition followed in 1726, when Newton was well over 80. As he neared the end of his life, Sir Isaac's brain stayed remarkably sharp. John Conduitt reported that he often witnessed his elderly uncle-by-marriage consumed with work in his elegant home.

Sir Isaac also kept his passion for the study of theology. During these London years, he wrote hundreds of pages about the history of the ancient Hebrews. The question of when life on Earth would end consumed him. He attended church, but he never revealed in public that he did not believe in the Trinity, the heresy that he had kept secret for 50 years.

Isaac Newton knew that he was a legend in his own time, and he worked to ensure that his reputation would live on. He sat for portraits with London's most gifted painters, and sculptors carved busts of him in marble. During his years in London, Newton continued to fight for his good name over that of Gottfried Leibniz in the priority dispute about calculus. To the very end, he fought to maintain his reputation as a natural philosopher, even when it meant staying embroiled in disagreements with Leibniz and Flamsteed for years and years.

Nevertheless, Newton appeared to humble himself when he declared:

> *I do not know what I may appear to the world; but to myself I seem to have been only like a boy playing on the seashore, and diverting myself in now and then finding a smoother pebble or a prettier shell than ordinary, whilst the great ocean of truth lay all undiscovered before me.*

There is no evidence that Isaac Newton ever saw the sea.

For a man who had spent three decades working with toxic materials in a laboratory, Isaac Newton had unusual good health. However, the day came when Sir Isaac's robust health began to go downhill. For his comfort, he decided to move west from London to the newly fashionable town of Kensington, where the air was less polluted.

Newton suffered from problems with his bladder, and he lost control of it. Jolting rides in a horse-drawn carriage aggravated the problem, but Newton was determined to stay on as president of the Royal Society. He bought a "sedan chair," a boxed-in seat with posts at both ends for two servants to carry him through London's streets. Even though he still was president, Newton began to nod off at Royal Society meetings. Meetings disintegrated into silly discussions about absurd subjects, just as they had before Newton took office.

In 1720 Newton suffered a blow to his personal fortune when he joined the frenzy of stock market investors who bought shares in the South Sea Company. From January through June, the stock's value grew from £128 to £1,050 per share. Newton invested £20,000 in the stock when it was at its peak—and lost it all when the infamous "South Sea Bubble" burst in September and shares dropped back to a mere £128 each.

But Newton kept working until the very end of his days. In March 1727, Sir Isaac presided over a regular meeting of the Royal Society in London. He was 84 years old. The meeting was to be his last. Returning home the next day, the elderly man took to his bed in terrible pain. A few days later he was dead. John Conduitt wrote about Newton's final hours and made a note of Sir Isaac's final act. It was the custom of Anglicans to receive the "sacraments" as they neared death, but Newton refused them. On March 20, 1727, Isaac Newton chose to meet God in his own way.

In the fashion of that era, a well-known sculptor came to Newton's home to take a "death mask" of Newton. The sculptor worked carefully as he poured wet plaster on the face of the dead scientist. Once it dried, the mask served as a mold to cast Newton's likeness. This death mask served as the model for later works of art showing the legendary man.

Newton's body lay in state in Westminster Abbey, surrounded by the tombs of England's kings and queens. His funeral was the grandest England had conducted for a natural philosopher. The very highest-born in England attended, looking on as Newton's pall was carried by nobles—two dukes and three earls who all were members of the Royal So-

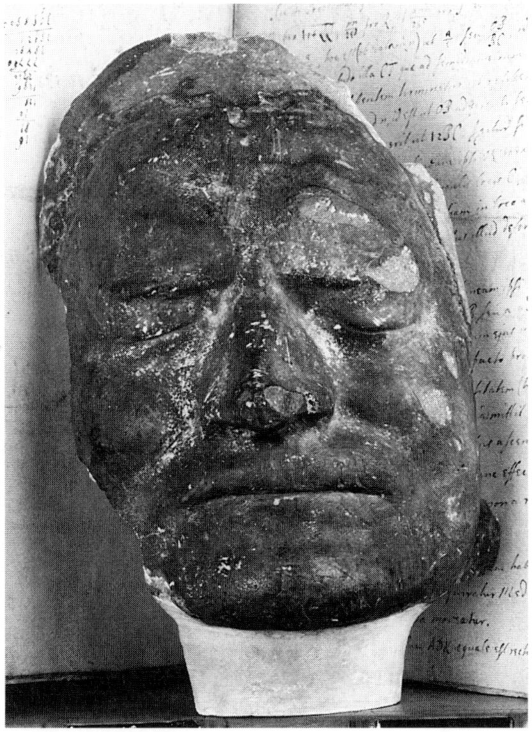

❖ Newton's death mask, placed in front of an original copy of the *Principia*. ©Jim Sugar

ciety. Newton's body was laid to rest beneath the floor in the western end of the Abbey, in front of his monument. Carved into the floor above were the Latin words *Hic depositum est, quod mortale fuit Isaaci Newtoni.* (Here lies that which was mortal of Isaac Newton.)

Looking at Newton through the Lens of History

Following his death, Isaac Newton got his wish: a legacy as one of history's most prominent scientists, if not one of the most famous people who ever lived. "Sir *Isaac Newton*, the greatest of Philosophers, and the Glory of the *British* Nation . . . ," wrote one newspaper reader. In death, Isaac Newton became larger than life. As Europe's nations grew ever stronger and began to colonize the world, the legacy of Isaac Newton became a point of national pride for English-speaking people.

Near his burial spot in Westminster Abbey, an ornate memorial of marble was installed a few years after his death. Poetic odes to the dead man were written, and people hung his portrait in their homes. Through-

✤ A monument to Isaac Newton stands near his grave in Westminster Abbey. Can you find the symbols that memorialize England's great scientist?

The Dean and Chapter of Westminster

out England, statues of the great man rose, including one in Grantham, where Newton had gone to school. On both sides of the Atlantic Ocean, in England and the American colonies, many baby boys were christened "Isaac Newton ______" for generations to come. People who knew Newton wrote about their memories of the great man in their diaries, and the first biographies about him started to appear.

Newton's manuscripts and letters were valuable, so people began to collect his papers and put them in safe places. Newton's relatives back in Woolsthorpe also hoped to gain control of Uncle Isaac's papers. Fearing that they wanted to sell them, John Conduitt outwitted the family and kept Newton's papers safe.

During the 1700s, "Newtonian mechanics" dominated the way scientists all across Europe and the Americas went about their work. Newton became a hero to the next generation of great intellectuals during the Enlightenment. Another term for this period of time is the "Age of Reason," when human knowledge blossomed.

Enlightenment thinkers like Voltaire, Benjamin Franklin, and Thomas Jefferson admired Newton. They saw him as a man of pure reason. To their way of thinking, Newton's science had ushered in a new age of wisdom and light that would push human progress to new heights. Alexander Pope, an English poet who often made fun of people, was deadly serious when he wrote about Newton:

Nature and Nature's Laws lay hid in night;
God said, 'Let Newton be!'—And all was light.

In the 1800s, a full century since Newton's death, Newton's biographers lionized him. They wrote flowery descriptions of his life, making Newton into a godlike figure. In sharp contrast, they wrote little about the dark side of Newton, his jealous personality and his quirky habits. Sometimes they found evidence of Newton's work in alchemy and religion that would have given him a bad name, so they covered it up, thinking that the public would never find out.

By the 1900s, historians began to take a more balanced view of Newton. Science had opened a new field of study called psychology, the study of the mind. It became popular to think about why people act as they do. As people began to understand more about human minds and emotions, biographers wrote about Newton's personality.

Now biographers looked not just at Newton's enormous scientific success but also at Newton the man. These historians wrote

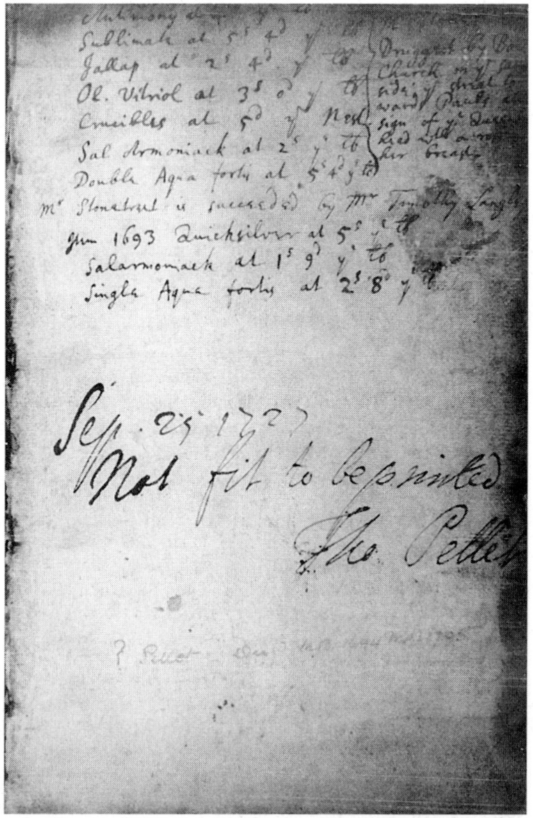

Sep. 25 1727
Not fit to be printed
Tho. Pellet

✤ "Not fit to be printed" declared a scholar who reviewed Newton's alchemical manuscripts soon after Newton's death. These manuscripts did not come to light for another two hundred years.

The Chymistry of Isaac Newton, Indiana University

✤ This statue of Isaac Newton stands at Cambridge University. Trinity College Library, Cambridge University

about Newton's jealous and unfair treatment of Hooke and Flamsteed. They criticized his bloody treatment of counterfeiters when he was master of the mint. Others questioned why Newton had so few friends in his Cambridge days. By the end of the 1900s, some writers were suggesting that Newton hid homosexual relationships he had with John Wickins and Fatio de Duillier.

In 1936 there arose a clue to Newton's secretive character. A huge collection of Newton's manuscripts was auctioned off in England and came into the hands of John Maynard Keynes, one of England's most famous economists. Keynes took the stacks of papers to read; what they contained surprised him. Some papers revealed that Newton had secretly practiced alchemy. Other papers confirmed that Newton did not believe in the Trinity and was afraid that others might find out.

This discovery added a major piece to the puzzle that was Isaac Newton. Researchers now had a much better picture of what he was doing during all his hidden years at Cambridge. This new information convinced Keynes that Newton wasn't a modern scientist. Instead, Keynes believed that Newton had "one foot in the Middle Ages and one foot treading a path for modern science." Keynes did not believe that Newton's work in alchemy had any scientific value at all.

But some scientists today disagree. Chemists are taking a careful look at Newton's manuscripts in alchemy with fresh eyes. These scientists suspect that Newton was just as interested in the chemical processes he studied in his laboratory as he was in their "magical" nature. They believe that Newton was in fact learning all he could about chemical technology and the behavior of metals. By building replicas of Newton's furnaces and reproducing his "chymistry," they hope to prove their case.

Newton's reputation as a great man of science stands firm. In fact, there are two "greatest minds" of science whom we think of today. One is Isaac Newton. The other is Albert Einstein, who revolutionized physics with his special and general theories of relativity in the early 1900s. Einstein's ideas carried science into a whole new realm of research when he asked what happens to moving objects as they approach the speed of light.

In 2005 the Royal Society held a contest for scientists and the public to choose "The Greatest Scientist Who Ever Lived." Scientists voted 61 percent for Newton and 39 percent for Einstein. The public split their vote: 50.1 percent for Newton and 49.9 percent for Einstein.

Einstein himself recognized Newton's powerful influence on physics. He declared

✤ Albert Einstein (1879–1955) Library of LC-USZC4-4940

that Newton was "a shining spirit who pointed out, as none before or after him did, the path of Western thought and research. . . ." As Einstein said, Newton's ideas about motion influenced all the other areas of physics: optics, the study of light; thermodynamics, the study of heat, energy, and gases; electricity and magnetism.

The life and work of Isaac Newton will always fascinate us. Massive amounts of Newton's writing still need study, and scholars will expand ideas about him for years to come. Even with all of the available evidence about Newton the man, questions will always remain, and scholars will continue making educated guesses about this mysterious but mortal human being.

William Wordsworth, England's great Romantic poet, offered a superb reflection on the mystery that shrouds Isaac Newton. Like Newton, Wordsworth attended Cambridge University. Wordsworth drew inspiration from a statue of Sir Isaac Newton, which Wordsworth said he could see from his bed.

The final line of Wordsworth's verse provides a strong visual image of Isaac Newton's inner life.

And from my pillow, looking forth by light
Of moon or favouring stars, I could behold
The antechapel where the statue stood
Of Newton with his prism and silent face,
The marble index [guide] *of a mind for ever*
Voyaging through the strange seas of
Thought, alone.

ACKNOWLEDGMENTS

My sincere thanks go to Dr. Robert Townsend of Xavier University, Dr. Ken Koehler of the University of Cincinnati, and my father, Frederick D. Logan, for lighting my way through the math and physics passages of this book. I also thank Brandon Marie Miller and Mary Kay Carson, who encouraged me to write about Newton, as well as Jerry Pohlen, my editor, who guided me through many an activity, and Martina Oroz, my student "tester." I am especially indebted to the members of my writing group for their careful review of the manuscript. My thanks to Amy Hobler, Diana R. Jenkins, Kathy Kitts, Geri Kolesar, Kellie Moster, and Lisa Murtha. Finally, every author needs a "cold" reader, and I'm grateful to my husband, Bill, whose pilot eyes see me through all kinds of weather.

RESOURCES

THERE ARE MANY ways to learn more about Isaac Newton, physics, and the history of science. One of the best is to visit the library where you live and ask a librarian to help you.

Following are some resources to get you started. Those marked with a "☙" are located in the children's or teens' department in the library.

Books

☙ Anderson, Margaret Jean. *Isaac Newton: The Greatest Scientist of All Time*. Springfield, NJ: Enslow Publishers, 2008.

☙ Boerst, William J. *Isaac Newton: Organizing the Universe*: Greensboro, N.C.: Morgan Reynolds Publishing, 2004.

☙ Carson, Mary Kay. *Exploring the Solar System: A History with 22 Activities*. Chicago: Chicago Review Press, 2006.

☙ Christianson, Gale E. *Isaac Newton and the Scientific Revolution*. New York: Oxford University Press, 1996.

Gleick, James. *Isaac Newton*. New York: Pantheon Books, 2003.

☙ Hakim, Joy. *The Story of Science, Aristotle Leads the Way*. Washington, DC: Smithsonian Books, 2004.

☙ Krull, Kathleen. *Isaac Newton*. New York: Viking, 2006.

Newton, Isaac. *Opticks: Or, a Treatise of the Reflections, Refractions, Inflections and Colours of (Designed by I. Bernard Cohen). New York: Dover Publications, 1952.*

Newton, Isaac, Sir. The *Principia : mathematical principles of natural philosophy / Isaac Newton ; a new translation* by I. Bernard Cohen and Anne Whitman assisted by Julia Budenz ; preceded by *A guide to Newton's Principia* by I. Bernard Cohen. Berkeley, CA.: University of California Press, 1999.

Panchyk, Richard. *Galileo for Kids: His Life and Ideas.* Chicago: Chicago Review Press, 2005.

Westfall, Richard S. *Never at Rest: A Biography of Isaac Newton.* New York: Cambridge University Press. 1980.

Westfall, Richard S. *The Life of Isaac Newton.* New York: Cambridge University Press, 1993.

Web Sites

Build a Newtonian Physics Machine
http://spaceplace.nasa.gov/en/kids/funphysics.shtml
This NASA Web site shows how to build a simple machine that illustrates Newton's Third Law.

The Chymistry of Isaac Newton
http://webapp1.dlib.indiana.edu/newton/
Chemists at Indiana University are researching Isaac Newton's alchemy and offer a new view of what Newton actually experienced in his laboratory. This Web site, a work in progress, offers a full transcription and online images of Newton's most complete laboratory notebook.

Cosmic Journey: A History of Scientific Cosmology
www.aip.org/history/cosmology/index.htm
A Web site presented by the American Institute of Physics with an excellent view of human study of the universe over time, as well as a thorough presentation of physics. Includes student and teacher resources.

Footprints of the Lion
www.lib.cam.ac.uk/Exhibitions/Footprints_of_the_Lion/
An online presentation of the Macclesfield Collection, purchased by the Cambridge University Library in 2000 for more than $12 million. The Macclesfield Collection

documents Sir Isaac Newton's writings and ideas, in letters and manuscripts, on gravitation, calculus, the *Principia mathematica*, optics, chemistry, comets and other subjects.

The Newton Project
www.newtonproject.sussex.ac.uk
This is the most comprehensive Web site of Isaac Newton's writings available online. A work in progress, its developers aim "to grasp the organic unity of Newton's writing by garnering all his astonishingly diverse productions into a single, freely accessible electronic edition."

***Newton's Dark Secrets* WGBH Boston Video, 2005.**
A *Nova* presentation about Isaac Newton including his practice of alchemy.

This video is enhanced by PBS's Web site, also titled Newton's Dark Secrets, at www.pbs.org/wgbh/nova/newton

The Physics Classroom Tutorial
www.physicsclassroom.com
A high school physics teacher has written this clear, useful online physics tutorial for introductory physics students.

INDEX

ISAAC NEWTON
1643-1727
$\Delta(mv)=F\Delta t$
DEUTSCHE
BUNDESPOST
100
1993

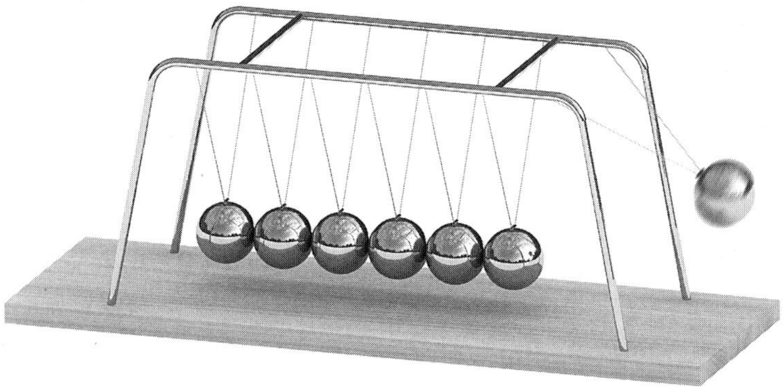

M

N

O

P

ISAAC NEWTON

Sir Isaac Newton
1642 : 1727